Building the Dream

By Lloyd Girardi
& Andi Cooke

Contents

Introduction

Welcome to our second book, Building the Dream.

What do we mean by "Building the Dream"? This is about people – regular people, just like you – from all walks of life, who found themselves curious, perhaps fascinated, by the idea of getting involved with property – more specifically, property developments – and who took that important first step to learn how better to build that dream. The people who share their stories here, in this book, are now, literally, building their dream and telling you how they did it.

This is what we at White Box Property Solutions do: We are property developers who teach others how to do what we've done – not just the successful parts but the missteps and, most importantly, how to avoid them, how to learn from our experience to make your path that much easier. Everyone interviewed in this book has come to us, at White Box Property Solutions, eager to find out more. They've taken one or more of our courses, joined our Mastermind and networking groups, some have participated in our personal development retreats, and each, as a result, has felt confident to start their own property development business.

They are excited by what they have then gone on to accomplish. Some are downright astonished by just how well they've done, how far they've come, and how fast. And they want to share their experiences with you.

Each chapter is a different story…

Who are we?

We are Lloyd Girardi and Andi Cooke, co-founders of White Box Property Solutions. We have become the UK's most successful property development educators, with an unparalleled reputation as comprehensive, generous, accessible educators and mentors.

We pride ourselves and our business on the success we create through the in-depth education we provide. We deliver our training the #whiteboxway – the way we wished we could have been taught when we were starting out.

We are candid; we are to the point. We highlight not just the success stories but also the potential obstacles that every developer – every developer – experiences at some point.

We are not interested in glossing over hurdles and painting a rosy picture. We want everyone who comes to us for help to know precisely what lies ahead on this path, how we have overcome the challenges and experienced the outcomes, and how they can do the same. Every challenge teaches us something on the path to success. By sharing the genuine challenges we and others in our network have faced is, we feel, the best way to learn. And through mentoring and our Mastermind, our students continue to get support. And as they learn and share, everyone benefits.

As our business grows, so do our students.

In 2018, we released our first book, Property Development, which was, and still is, a huge success. Property Development takes you through the first four years of our property journey, from our initial start in 2014, when we had zero money, time, or knowledge of how to do what we wanted to do, and takes you through to 2018, at which point we had developed numerous sites, from big conversions to new builds.

Property Development provides practical advice and real-life experiences to help you get started. In fact, many of the individuals who share their stories in this book, as you will soon discover, began their journey by reading our first book, Property Development, and went on from there. It inspired them to act.

Education is a catalyst to success.

Everyone has a story. Everyone and every story is different. But the common thread is that each of these individuals learned that anyone can become a property developer – if you are prepared to put in the work.

What is worth doing is worth doing well. Knowledge is power. You've heard this before. Because it's true.

Developments are not effortless – true success and building your personal legacy never is. But it is achievable.

Developments are challenging, but that's precisely what makes them so fun and rewarding. And they are what fill us with a genuine sense of accomplishment, including the contribution we're making to our communities.

When we speak to those who have expressed interest but are hesitating, we hear the same reasons, the same perceptions, over and over again:

Fear

Risk

Lack of Money

Lack of Education

Lack of Knowledge/Experience

Mindset

Lack of Belief

Lack of Credibility

Lack of Time

We understand. We've been there ourselves. We know what it feels like. The only difference between us and them is that we have identified these perceptions – and they are perceptions, not insurmountable obstacles. We have identified these concerns within ourselves, addressed them, and overcome them. And so has everyone who shares their story in this book.

You are the only person standing in your way, the only one who's stopping you from becoming a success, from building your dream.

Are you ready?

May we suggest that you read this book not in one sitting but one chapter at a time. Take some time after each to think about the story you've just read. Think carefully. Ask yourself:

Does that sound like me?

If it does, use the contact information we provide to reach

out to that individual, or those partners, and engage with them. Speak to them. Networking is a huge part of successful developments. Learn from people who have done it, are doing it, and are willing to help you do the same.

And keep reading. Keep reading about their journeys, their successes and challenges, told in their own words.

And then reach out to us. We're here to help.

In fact, we want to help you get started that much, we have put together a collection of our most valuable videos and content that you can gain access to right now... (or maybe after you've read the book)

Just scan the QR code below and indulge in some of our most inspirational videos.

MATT KAVANAGH – FRONT ROW DEVELOPMENTS

http://www.frdevelopments.com/

https://m.facebook.com/frdevelopments/?tsid=0.42646637531088794&source=result

Instagram - @frdevelopments

TikTok - @frdevelopments

In this chapter we talk to Matt Kavanagh. Initially, it was Matt's dad, Ian, who approached White Box. Ian attended one of our property network events in 2017, wanting to do something more in property. After buying a few HMOs around the country, he wanted a bigger challenge and wanted to bring his son Matt into the business.

Matt and Ian converted an old doctors surgery into seven apartments when they first joined White Box. That development was good experience, but the education from White Box spring-boarded them into what has become a hugely successful development business.

Fast forward to today, about five years after having started with us, Matt is now a White Box mentor and helps other people get started just like he did, and just like we did in 2014. Matt is more than qualified to help people in our eyes now, as he has developed, and is developing, 10 sites in total. Ian has now stepped back from the business to work on his golf game and focus on getting his handicap down to single digits.

They will tell you that a big turning point for them was when they attended our Business and Personal Development Retreat in Bali in 2019. We gave them a tangible plan to follow and pursue. In fact, at the time of this writing, we are currently in Croatia, on our Business and Personal Development Retreat, with Matt and Ian yet again participating.

"It's my absolute pleasure", Andi says with a smile, "to welcome Matt Kavanagh to the podcast".

"Thanks for having me", Matt says. "Things are going well. We had our overall group meeting last week to set us up for the year, to set our goals – what we want to achieve. It's exciting to get that set."

"Yes," Lloyd says. "As Andi said, it's a pleasure to have you here. We're looking forward to getting into the details of what you've achieved in the time we've known you. You're a veteran now, on our Mastermind. How long have you been with us so far?"

"I think it's coming up to three years, now. I suspect I'm the longest running in the group", he says, grinning.

"Certainly, you're one of the longest", Andi says, nodding. "We've got a few who have been on for a good while. It's difficult when you're just getting started, but as you start to gain momentum and get some traction, deals start coming to you and you build your bank of investors." He laughs. "In your case though, I remember that it was your dad who came to the three-day Property Developers Secrets course to test the waters, to see what it was all about. He got you into it. Tell us about that part of your journey, how it all happened, what you were thinking at the time, what you wanted to get out of the course. And after that, we'll get to the results you've experienced."

Matt nods. "We'd been doing property of a sort since 2015. I'd started as a letting agent, an estate agent, a mortgage broker, and transitioned through various companies, and was a commercial finance broker when I came on the White Box course.

"The plan had always been to build up income to where I could exit my job and focus on property full-time. We'd been investing, and, typically, at some point, you start running out of available cash. We thought, well, let's get into developments, where we can generate cash, which we can then invest, and keep the momentum going.

"We started looking around and secured our first development site in about 2018, I think it was. We got halfway through, at which point things weren't going according to plan – when it's your first site, there's always plenty to learn.

"By then, my father had attended your one-day introductory course, heard you speak about your network, decided straight away to do the White box three-day course, and came off that very excited, saying, 'I've got to do that again!' and registered for the very next one.

"That's what changed our property journey, from our original approach which was that development was secondary, just a means to an end, where we might do one every few years to boost our available cash, to where it's now the main thing that we do, and it's the investment side that has now become secondary. About six months after we started the Mastermind, I was finally able to quit my job and commit wholly to doing property. The mentoring really made a difference, transitioning us from doing it on the side to doing it full-time. Originally getting involved with White Box started off as an insurance policy of sorts, to make sure we didn't screw up that first development too badly, but we've stuck with it." He grins. "We've never been apart since!"

Lloyd smiles. "I remember your dad on the course. He's a very shrewd businessman, very savvy. He gets what business is about, and property development is a business. I remember him coming up and saying, 'Oh, I've got to get my son on this. I've got to get my son to come along and have a look.' So, tell us, how many sites have you currently got in your portfolio in terms of secured, completed, in the planning stage?"

Matt glances at a large whiteboard to his left that lists the various projects he's got underway.

"In addition to the three sites we've completed, start to finish, we've got seven more sites in the pipeline: some in the planning stage, some we're currently building out, and a few finishing off the legal phase so we can submit planning. Probably enough to keep us busy for the next three years, but we'll keep trying to add to it. We try to ensure we're always ready to act on anything good that might come our way."

"That's impressive", Lloyd says. "Ten deals is phenomenal, especially given that when you came to us, you weren't yet sure if it was right for you."

"Yeah", Matt says with a chuckle. "It turns out it was pretty right for us!"

"Another win in this is that your dad has since been able to pretty much retire from the hands-on end of the business, hasn't he? He's pursuing other interests now, right? I know he does a lot of trading and stuff now, having been able to turn over the day-to-day running of your property and development business to you, which he couldn't do before, and allow you to run it. He oversees it, still spends time on it, but now", Andi says with a grin, "he has time to do something else he's wanted to do: to get in a bit more golf and get his handicap down".

"It's always been a big part of the plan", Matt agrees, "to grow the business to a point where he could step away for most of the week, and spend it playing golf. Plus, my brother and his family are over in Australia, so he likes to visit them. Obviously, the pandemic got in the way of that, but he'd like to spend a couple of months a year in Australia without it being a handicap for the business. It's nice to be at that point now."

"We'll touch on how you got there", Lloyd says, "and how it all started, but, first, what are we looking at GDV-wise, the gross development value? What's the anticipated profit from the deals you're looking at?"

"In terms of what we have in the pipeline", Matt says, glancing at the whiteboard again, "most of the deals are pretty much the same – we're working at a similar sort of level. At the moment, overall GDV is about £20 million and profit around £4 million."

"Impressive! So, when you say they're similar, you mean that they're similar in terms of the number of units? Or similar-sized units?"

"Yes, similar-sized units, so the GDV on each site is roughly the same. If one is slightly bigger in size, it might not be quite as good an area, or if it's in an affluent village location, it might be smaller but higher priced. So, yes, they're all sitting at around £2.5 million GDV. That seems to be our sweet spot.

"This approach streamlines that whole process as, even though each deal is individual, we know what we're looking at from a lending point of view, and from an investor point of view. They know the type of thing they can expect going forward. So, when we speak to potential investors, we have a pretty good idea of what a typical deal will look like even before we've got a specific one to share with them."

Andi chuckles. "So, back when your dad was telling you to check out our three-day course, did you ever envision that, in three years' time, you'd have a pipeline of £20 million worth of GDV? Of £4 million pounds worth of profit? You being able to leave behind your job, all those things you just talked about – did you conceive of that? Was that your plan at the time? What did you see in terms of your direction?"

"It's gone way better than we ever thought it would", Matt admits. "We talked about momentum a moment ago, and it was surprising to us how far the first and second deals took us. Once you start to build up momentum, it's amazing the things that come to you.

"We've had a couple of deals", he adds, "from people we've known for years, the difference being that they now know that's what we do. They've seen what we've done and now they're picking up the phone and telling us about a parcel somewhere. It creates that flow, once people know what you do – they've seen you do X, Y, and Z. It's hard to explain how much of a difference that makes. It really does. I think we probably had six months on a Mastermind where not an awful lot happened in terms of new deals, and then, suddenly, we got three deals in the subsequent six months."

"That's actually pretty normal", Lloyd says. "Not necessarily that you'd get three deals in six months, because it does take time, but once the flow starts, opportunity comes. A lot of people might not realise that sometimes it does take time to get that initial momentum. That's what we try and teach you at White Box: the realities of it." Lloyd smiles. "What you're saying makes it sound rosy. It all sounds great: you've got 10 sites, £20 million GDV, but it wasn't always that easy, not from the start. It takes time. There are often complications along the way. Let's talk now about a few of the challenges you encountered along the way."

Matt smiles ruefully, rubbing his chin. "We have had a few tough ones, yes. We had three where they had agreed to sell but pulled out on the day of exchange, where we just got an email from their solicitor that said, 'I've been instructed not to proceed', that they'd be proceeding with someone else, and that was it – they never picked up the phone again, when we literally had the money and solicitors ready to go.

"It's about understanding that these kinds of things can and do happen. That's the nature of developments. People will unexpectedly drop in and out of things, and decide they want to do something else. What we learned early on from that was that, yes, we'd committed a lot of time and energy to something, but when this happens, you've got to be philosophical about it, to let them go and move on. There will always be another deal, so if this one wasn't meant to be, it wasn't meant to be.

"I think of it as more of a numbers game. You can't put all of your energy into one thing, because if you do and that one thing gets pulled out on the day of exchange, all you'll think about is what a waste of three months it's been, or whatever.

It's important to have a pipeline, to have a number of deals at any one time, in various stages."

"Don't get emotional, at least not until the very end", Lloyd warns with a smile, "only when it's completed, which is when relief kicks in".

"Yes", says Andi, "it's important to find a balance, to temper the excitement of finding a deal, along with any potential disappointment that could occur, and keep more of an even keel. I remember you telling us that your first deal, Lansdowne Road, had some issues, which was one of the core reasons your dad took the White Box course. It was an insurance policy, of sorts, to quote you, to make sure you mitigated the risk and controlled the downside. It wasn't a 100% success but, nonetheless, you said it provided so much momentum – it got you known as a developer. It got you your second and third deals, so you got traction from it. That's important for people who are going through, or even just nervously contemplating, their first deal to hear that it does get easier. You just got to stick with it. You only fail if you give up."

"It definitely gives you overall credibility", Matt says, "especially when dealing with agents. Quite often they'll ask, 'What have you done locally?' So, being able to point to a few projects we've completed gets you a foot in the door, as they can see that you're active, that you've finished something. Getting that first deal done gives you that credibility to find future projects."

"What advice would you give anyone who hasn't got that track record, or wants to get started?" Lloyd asks.

Matt thinks a moment.

"Well, we had our first project underway before we took the White Box course, but my advice would be: The quicker you can build a track record, the better. And I think there are two ways to do it. One is that you build it quickly and just get a deal done – it doesn't need to be the biggest project. So, if you're bidding against 30 other people for a 10-unit site early on, it might be best to just go and get one small-sized deal done, a single house or two houses, even if it's not the type of deal you want to do going forward. Getting started, learning and understanding the process, going through that process, finishing a development, along with all the things that are attached to that, is invaluable. So, doing your first one on a smaller scale is not a bad option.

When we first started, because we wanted to get on with it quickly, our focus was to look at stuff already on the market, with planning in place, generally. For us, it was more of a timescale issue, whereas, now, most of the stuff we look at is off-market, because now we've got the luxury of our existing project pipeline to afford us the ability to wait a couple of years before we start building something. If you were just starting out and went for a site with no planning, it could be three years easily before you could start, such as if there are obstacles with the local council."

"That's the thing", Lloyd says. "A lot of people think the best deals are the ones that you've found off-market, that you've got planning on there, and you've bought cheaply. While they could well be decent deals, it could take three or four years to complete it.

"I worked out the stat the other day", he adds, "that 85% of the deals that Andi and I have done have been on Rightmove, at least at some point. So, deals are out there. You've just got to pay what it's worth to you and no more. I would advise ignoring any asking price on Rightmove and just offer what you can pay."

"Certainly, the deals that we've got on Rightmove and similar, we've never paid what they've asked for", Matt says, nodding.

"No one does", Lloyd agrees.

"And I think that putting together the offer package, which we learned how to do from the White Box course, is an advantage, as it gives the agent and the vendor more information to work with. If nothing else, it's a conversation starter. Our offer package, while possibly not as detailed as some others I suspect, kicks off that conversation, where we can meet the owner or whomever, and gives us a better chance to make a deal.

"And it's important to remember", Matt adds, "that it's a people business. People will sell to you if they like you. Of course, the rest of it's got to fit as well, in terms of having the money in place, and the expertise to deliver. But, really, it's essentially a people business, and if you can get in front of people, then you've got a better chance at convincing them that you can do the deal."

"Absolutely", Lloyd says. "Any business is ultimately about relationships, but development, certainly. We always say that you're never the one doing all the work; you're the conductor who's orchestrating who's doing the work. And that means you're dealing with people every single day, whether it's your architect, your builder, your solicitor, your investors – you've got to be cordial and agreeable. If there's any animosity between any of you, the deal won't get done, at least not efficiently. It's a very relationship-based business."

"Couldn't agree more", Matt says. "It's about building trust, because you can't build a relationship without that, can you? And building your network. We might, before we go look at a site, have someone mention, 'Oh, we're not really sure what we're doing with X, Y and Z trees'. And I'll say, 'Why don't I send our tree surgeons around and they can have a look and see what they think, to see if we might need to go to the council and get licences, or whether we can just get on with it?' We're happy to do that. Anything, just to be helpful."

"The Law of Reciprocity", Lloyd says, "which is to help someone out without expecting anything in return, as, invariably, the goodwill comes back to you eventually."

"We're always very open, very honest about what we're trying to put on the site", Matt says. "We wouldn't claim that we're going to put three houses on a site and then slap in an application for 10 houses. It's about being open and honest, and dealing with people in a way that you'd want to be dealt with."

"I remember when your dad first came on the course", Andi says, "one thing that really resonated with me, something I really liked about him, was that he wasn't just trying to help himself in this endeavour. He wasn't even just trying to help the two of you, your family, whatever. Instead, he saw it as an opportunity for everyone on your team to grow together. That included your building contractor and all the people working together, and on the site as well. When you were doing HMOs, you were using a builder whom you knew from school. He'd grown with you, going from being a simple builder doing extensions to doing bigger stuff with you. Your dad wanted him on your journey and ensure he profited from it, as well as everyone else. That continues to be your approach, even now, while you're doing £20 million in GDV."

"Absolutely", Matt says, nodding. "And we're going to be joint-venturing with him now, for the first time, so that that'll be good for him. We'd done a lot of conversions from houses into HMOs, and he had done all of those with us, but full-blown development was definitely a step up for him. And we had got a few other builders to price it, but when we sat down to decide what we wanted to do with it, we realised we'd rather have Dom do it, because we trust him to be honest, to be level with us, to look after us, rather than a builder we didn't really have a relationship with. Another builder might have been better qualified in some ways, because he's delivered similar projects, but we felt we'd rather go on that journey with Dom, because of the trust element. It's so valuable to have someone on-site all the time whom you know, whom you can trust to look after you."

"And", Andi says, "it frees you up to go off and find more deals, which why you've got such a strong pipeline, knowing that you can trust him to do the development side of it. If you were to keep getting bigger sites without bringing him along to play a bigger role, you risk generating animosity, where he's getting resentful thinking, 'Well, you guys are making all the money, and I'm just getting a percentage bit.' This way, it allows you to grow together, doesn't it?"

"Unquestionably", Matt says. "He's grown his business to align with the roughly £8 million worth of build costs we've got lined up for over the next few years, so he can look after those sites. It works well for everyone."

"We always advise to look at those around you to see who you can share the journey with", Lloyd notes. "And it is a journey – there are a lot of ups and downs, a lot of crossroads, a lot of things that can go wrong as well as right. But you've done really well. We have three key points we stress at White Box to succeed: 1) be friendly, 2) be personable, and 3) be honest in your dealings. And we've seen you exemplify this, which is why, in the month after we're recording this, you're slated to join White Box as a mentor, teaching other people how to get started.

"Choosing you to do this, to join us as a mentor, isn't a decision we took lightly", Lloyd adds. "You've done 10 deals now, you've been through the process amply, you've experienced both ups and downs, all of which is key to truly helping other people follow in your footsteps and adding value."

"I'm really looking forward to getting started. I've spent nearly three years participating, and have probably heard it all", Matt says, grinning. "I've listened to numerous discussions of different issues and queries, and am anticipating sharing some of our experiences, the ups and downs we've had, in the hopes that it will help others, as you say. This journey is never a straight line, no matter how much it might look like it is. But that's what makes it exciting."

Lloyd nods. "So, tell us: What are your plans for the future?"

"Our focus this year is delivering the pipeline, but to possibly add a couple of new deals to it. We're quite happy continuing with the size we're doing versus moving into bigger and bigger projects. We know what we're good at doing, which gives us roughly a two- to three-year timescale, start to finish, on each site, which is not too bad and provides sufficient cash for everything we're doing. I'm enjoying the process, so no reason to change things for now."

Andi leans forward. "What about financial goals? You came to one of our retreats and that was a key point – you came out to Bali as a family and set some goals: your dad wanted to free himself up to play more golf, you had your eye on getting a Land Rover, which you've done... Any other checkpoints you're looking at?"

"Well", Matt says, "there are some financial goals that we're still working on since Bali, most of which will be accomplished when we deliver the current pipeline. What takes up most of Dad's time is the pension-fund side of things. We're looking to top that pot up and grow it long term.

"The cash flow side of things is, how we would employ our cash, hasn't really changed. Whenever I hear any of us talking about a cash flow goal, it seems to be in the region of £10 grand a month, and ours is pretty similar – except that's what each of us wants", he adds, chuckling. "That's what we're working towards. We've got a pretty good idea of what it's going to take to get there, and if we deliver this pipeline, we won't be a million miles away from that!"

"It really gives Andi and I a sense of pride to see you doing what you're doing, as we've been with you almost from the start on your journey. And your journey has been impressive."

"Your help is always much appreciated", Matt says.

"We're looking forward to having you in the Mastermind program", Andi adds, "as I'm sure we'll be able to support a lot of people in their journeys."

"And here's to the next three years", Lloyd says.

STUART DAVIES – NEIL STUART HOMES

www.neilstuarthomes.co.uk

Stuart has been very successful in his first development after training with White Box. He did exactly what we taught and he got a site very quickly. In fact, we helped Stuart get the funding he needed for his first development by introducing him to one of our investors. With White Box, we're all about sharing the journey with people, and helping them out, as much as we are about doing our own developments.

Stuart did his first development whilst working a full-time job too. Don't let that stop you from getting started. Being a developer is the same as being a conductor – you aren't expected to play all the instruments, just like you aren't expected to do the architect's work, the builder's work, the solicitor's work, and so on. What you need to do to be successful is to simply put the right people in the right place and oversee the process.

This is exactly what Stuart did.

"Today we're talking to Stuart Davies", Lloyd says. "When we were filming our 'Building the Dream' series, which can be viewed on YouTube, we visited Stuart's site and filmed a portion of it there."

We've got a strong community at White Box", says Andi, "so it's great to catch up with you, Stuart, as one of the people who has attended our course and is now out there successfully doing development. You also came to one of the White Box retreats."

"Now, these interviews", Lloyd explains, "in book form, are being published to provide greater detail to those just getting started, so before we delve into your background, would you share with us first what you've achieved development-wise since you started?"

Stuart nods. "Well, the first site we did was in Pocklington, and that had a GDV, a gross development value, of £1.42 million. Estimated profit from the development at initial writing was about £300,000, and the land was £300,000. Currently, we're looking at our next site in Wakefield, and we have another in the pipeline in York. That's what I've done thus far, since first taking your course and then going to the retreat in Bali."

"And how did you get started?", Lloyd asks. "What made you think about becoming a property developer, to take that leap? What was your background at the time?"

"I tried to get in the Royal Marines when I was younger", Stuart explains, "and I failed. That was my goal in life, to be a Royal Marine. And so, when I came out of the trials for the Marines, my dad said to me, 'You need to go and get a trade'. So, I became a plumber by trade, on construction sites, and then became a site supervisor, in charge of the plumbers. But I wanted something different. I was putting in a lot of hours, I was getting up and traveling to London, to Newcastle, and was away from the family a lot. I decided I wanted to get into property, but what, I didn't know – maybe single-let or serviced accommodation. I didn't have a clue. I just wanted a change.

"So, I started by doing a little bit of training with another real estate company, but nothing really resonated with me. I'd say probably about after a year of looking and researching, a light bulb went off and I started thinking, well, I don't know how to build houses, but I work on construction sites, and maybe going down the development side would be the right route for me.

"So, I did a bit more research and I found White Box. Not knowing who you were or anything about you, I wanted to do more research on you, rather than just going all in." He chuckles. "I sort of stalked a few people who had taken your courses, and not one had a bad word to say, which is very rare! I mean, among training companies you might find five or so people who have negative things to say, but no one had anything remotely negative to say about White Box. I thought, if that's the case, I need to look into this more, which I did. I bit the bullet, started with your one-day course, and it spiralled from there."

"The one-day course", Lloyd explains, "is our Property Developers Discovery Day, a one-day introduction to help interested people decide whether they want to take it further. The idea is to give them an easier option than our three-day course, one where they can decide first whether development is something they want to do or not, without too much of an investment.

"A lot of that one-day course", Lloyd adds, "is an honest depiction of the kinds of challenges one faces in doing developments, the ups and downs, and illustrates the reality that, if you can do it, there are rewards at the end." Lloyd smiles. "You are, obviously, proof that it can be done."

"It bears repeating", Stuart says, "what you said about it

being honest. Rather than gloss over the tough questions, you went into great detail in your answers. I don't think anyone went away with some sort of woolly, vague answer – it was all nail-on-the-head stuff, which was excellent value."

"We've been training those interested in becoming developers for a good few years now", Andi says. "It didn't take long before we realised that people are more successful when they hear the realities, when they learn of the potential obstacles, some of the challenges that we've hit doing our own developments, and how we tackled those issues.

"You can't just paint a rosy picture", Andi adds, "because development is not like that." He chuckles. "We're different people than who we were when we started, and I'm sure you've changed too, since starting your journey. Challenges aren't necessarily bad though. It brings out your creativity. They're an opportunity to learn, and learn we do, and usually at a quicker rate than if nothing on our previous sites ever went wrong. If that were to happen, it'd be so unlikely as to be a false reality.

"We want people to be prepared for what lies ahead", Andi says, "on the road to success. Were everything on your first site to go without so much as a glitch, you'd go headlong into a second site, assuming everything would go just as smoothly, and arguably get yourself into a much worse position. We learn from challenges and that experience. So, from day one, we tell people the way it really is. That one-day course is not just a financial investment but an investment of your time. We don't want you to waste your time. And the course is only the first step. You've got to take the information and move forward with it, implement it. To be a developer is quite a journey, quite a commitment, wouldn't you say?"

"Well, our first site went very well, but we certainly did have hiccoughs", Stuart admits, "but we were determined to overcome them and we did. I can guarantee that, on the next site we do, we'll have similar hiccoughs. Maybe not so much the same ones we had the first time, as we learned from them, but there will be challenges. It's been a good journey, though, an exciting journey."

"You said earlier that, on paper, you had anticipated a £300,000 profit", Lloyd notes. "But the realities of developing mean they aren't always realised. Tell us about that deal. How did you find it? We'll talk about the funding in a moment, but how did you initially find it?"

"It was funny, actually", Stuart admits. "I was working at University of York, overseeing the work of a heating installation company. One of the company's directors, Neil, casually asked me what I was doing that weekend, and I told him I was going on a three-day course with a company called White Box. Curious, he started asking me questions about what kind of course. I said I wanted to become a developer, which led to even more questions, and I admitted that I was thinking about leaving the university job, as I didn't like the hours and was looking for something else. About a week later, he gave me a call and invited me to come to his office for a chat, saying he'd tell me what it was about when I got there.

"I immediately suspected he was going to offer me a job, but instead he took me to see this plot of land and said, 'I know the owner of this site. He's thinking of selling. Would you want to come in together with me?' He knew I was doing the White Box three-day training course, so he was proposing a partnership, for us to create a company.

I thought, whoa, I need to get training first. I can't just jump in and do this. So, I went to the three-day course, and it all clicked. So, technically, I found the site before I took the course. But I wasn't in any position to do anything with it until after I'd taken the course and knew more not just about how to do it but having affirmed that I wanted to do it. It's something you kept repeating throughout the course: the importance of networking, of telling everyone what you do, no matter who they are and what they do. If I hadn't told him I was coming on a three-day White Box course to learn how to become a developer, he would never have shared that opportunity with me. So, you could say that it was a very good coincidence", he said with a shrug, "but I don't believe in coincidences".

"And that goes back to one of our favourite sayings...", Lloyd says with a grin.

"Tell everyone what you do", Andi says, finishing Lloyd's thought.

"Well, not everything!", Lloyd exclaims.

Laughter.

"That was very brave of you, Stuart", Andi adds, "putting yourself out there before you'd even done the training – telling people that you're going to do it. Lloyd and I discussed the topic of imposter syndrome in another interview, how hard it can be not just to step up to the next level but how intimidating it can be to go out and tell people you know about your wanting to take on a totally new venture." He chuckles. "Not unlike when you start going to the gym out of the blue, and you're far from being a bodybuilder or anything like that. You hesitate telling people until you know you're going to stick with it and start to see results. It's very much the same as becoming a developer. And there's always the risk of a negative reaction. Not everyone is supportive. Sad to say, not everyone wants to see people succeed, people who are taking a risk, stepping outside their comfort zone to improve their lot. People might say, well, you can't be a developer – you don't have any experience! But don't let that stop you. Any conversation is potentially a good conversation, because you just don't know where it's going to lead."

"That's so true", Stuart says with a wry grin. "When I first shared this goal with my friends and family – that I was going to do these courses to become a developer – the reactions were all negative. Now, however, everyone's fascinated. 'How did you learn to do that? Where did you get the money from?' I have to admit that it's quite a nice feeling to see them responding positively, even admiringly, not negatively. Positivity makes such a difference, doesn't it?"

Lloyd nods. "I reckon every single person listening to this, or reading this, has had exactly the same experience at some point. Not necessarily in development, but anytime you try and do something different, maybe a little ambitious, there always seems to be someone who casts doubt on what you're capable of doing, or how you are going to do it, or the process behind it. We see it a lot with developments. People assume it's impossible to get started unless you've already accumulated a load of money and have experience. The education part helped, obviously, but we can't do it for you. You chose to take what you learned and take action. You did it, and you completed it successfully. You have to get past that negativity of people, just ignore it to start with. Everyone's going to encounter it, without a doubt."

Stuart chuckles. "Some of those who were really negative initially are now asking me where I went to do the training!"

"And you came to one of our retreats", Lloyd points out, "the one in Bali, one of our business retreats. That was a big decision for you, wasn't it, because you don't like flying. Yet, a part of you knew that you would benefit from going, so you overcame that fear and flew to Bali. You had, in the forefront of your mind, what you were looking to do, and funding was an issue at the time, wasn't it?"

"It was, yes, my two big concerns. The big F's: flying and funding. And they were long flights, too. My dad dropped me off at Newcastle Airport – I had to fly from Newcastle to Dubai, which was about eight hours, and then Dubai to Bali, which was about another nine hours, I think."

He shakes his head. "I had a bit of a panic attack as we were boarding, in the little tunnel you go through to board the flight. I had tears my eyes; I was shaking. I hated it. I was on my own, as well, so I had no one to talk to, to distract me. But, ultimately, the flights weren't as bad as I'd feared, and it's certainly helped reduce my reluctance to fly. So, yes, my two big challenges then were flying and funding, but funding was the biggest issue.

"So, here we were, with this site. I knew how to raise finance, because I learned at White Box how to raise maybe 65–75%, which I did, but I didn't know how to raise the equity portion. And I needed that extra money, which I didn't have, to complete the development. So, Bali, to me, was a game changer."

"The whole idea of Bali", Lloyd says, "was to help you with your business, but even more so to help you with the development. But one thing we talked about there was this site. The Bali retreat is a very intimate sort of experience, which goes on for seven days, where we're talking in detail about people's lives and livelihoods – all sorts of things. So, when you were there, you parsed through this deal with all of us around the table, sharing the thought process behind it, the due diligence you did. And someone at that table, who happens to be one of our big investors, expressed an interest in investing in your deal to cover the equity portion. Right there, at that table, he said, 'I'll fund that part for you.' Talk about a life-changing moment!"

"Yes, it was very emotional", Stuart admits. "I couldn't believe that he was willing to do that, make that commitment right then. It's so true that you don't get answers unless and until you put it out there.

"There are people that, say, go on Facebook, and write, 'I've got a deal here, and I need [this much] equity'. That's all well and good, and I'm sure sometimes they do get investors that way, investors they don't know", Stuart says. "But I expect that when I meet an investor who doesn't know who I am, I would want them to feel confident that they would have a good relationship with me, that there was some synergy between us. They're not going to lend me money on our first meeting, or the second, or the third, or even the fifth, because it takes a long time to gain that trust. They would need to feel comfortable with me as well as me feeling comfortable with them.

"But I found that the atmosphere at the Bali retreat condensed that process. As you say, we were all sat about the table, getting to know each other, learning everyone's past history:

we drank together, we ate together, we discussed business together. And that had the effect of condensing maybe 10 coffee meetings over the space of six months into a single week.

"So, yeah, you can certainly say that being at the Bali retreat 100% changed my life. And the investor we're talking about, a lovely bloke – we have that synergy. I message him probably every other week now, just to see how he is, not just to see if he might be interested in doing another development. So, I gained a friendship there, as well as an investor."

Andi nods. "We hear this a lot, that the retreats – and we do one in Croatia, as well – are a really big growth experience for everyone involved. 'A life-changing experience' is a phrase we frequently hear from participants, something that's quite humbling for us, and that the environment is, as you say, that condensed atmosphere that breaks down barriers. The way that it's set up, everyone's very open and honest, and that expedites everything. It's a big factor in why our return rate is something like 80–85%, where participants want to repeat that experience, who are to take their business to the next level and build again."

"So", Lloyd says, "going back to the three-day Property Developer Secrets course that you did after having done our introductory one-day course, people are typically curious about the quality of the information you get, and whether you get continuing support after the course is over. We, of course, also offer the Mastermind program to do just that, but you felt confident enough after just the three-day course to move forward with developing the site you had, even before Bali."

"That's correct", says Stuart. "When I took the three-day

course, I felt you'd left no stone unturned, and so I came away ready to start doing developments. I had set my mind to it, went off, and implemented what I'd been taught. It's like teaching someone how to be a plumber: you can give them the tools and show them how to do it, but if they don't take that next step and go out and do it, they're not going to make any money, because they're not using what they've learned. You can, without a doubt, take the three-day course and get started doing developments after that, just like I did. It gave me enough traction to feel ready to move forward. Bali, later on, was a further springboard for me in terms of my challenge to find funding, but Bali's not just about funding", he emphasises. "There were other people there who had other challenges and came away having got massive benefits in how to handle those individual challenges because of the personal, individual sharing and attention, the roundtable discussions. I would definitely go back again, and that's me, hating to fly!"

Laughter

"Don't make it sound like a holiday", Lloyd warns, grinning. "It's anything but a holiday! We do some serious hard work there!

"So", Lloyd continues, "let's look at the positives of your having done that site, as you've finished the deal now. And if anyone wants to see the site we're talking about, check out our YouTube channel. So, what's next for you, Stuart? What, for example, have you done with the profits? Have you invested them into something else? Or have you done a little something nice for yourself?"

"I had a little bit of debt, about £1,000, accrued from when I was younger, so some of my share of the profits paid those off. The remaining profit is still in the business, targeted towards our next site, which is in Wakefield: four large detached houses. We're waiting for the vendor on that to get an indemnity policy, an insurance policy against a small slither of land – we should have that this week. And we also had a meeting with a guy in York whose family business owns a plot of land, one which is quite exciting actually. We haven't financially committed to it, but he's a friend of a friend, so there is a connection there. We've had an email from him and his mother saying that they will sell that land to us when the time is right, hopefully within a year and a half. That's quite a large scheme, one I've put to the investor I met in Bali and he's extremely keen on it as well, having looked at the figures. So, we're just waiting until the time is right on that one."

"Forgive me for briefly turning this into a mentoring session", Lloyd interjects, "but this is the first time we've heard about this, so I'm just reminding you to get the option agreement secure on that, so you are guaranteed the option to buy later on; otherwise, they could change their minds and leave you hanging."

"That's good advice. I'll do that", Stuart promises. "So, that's it. We've got York in the pipeline, hopefully in a year and a half; we've got Wakefield that we hopefully will get over the line this week in terms of the insurance policy; and my having paid off some personal debt, all from the profits of that first development."

"That's awesome", Lloyd says. "So, tell us: thinking back, what was your biggest fear about getting into property development?"

Stuart thinks for a moment.

"I'd have to say it was the prospect of failure. Failure was something I'd experienced before. I had England trials when I was a young lad, at rugby, in the under eighteens, but I never got in – I'd played for the north of England; I tried to get in the Royal Marines and I failed at that; and after the Royal Marines, I tried to get on the oil rigs, and I failed at that too. So", he says, chuckling ruefully, "it felt like everything I tried was just going wrong. And it was the prospect of making the financial commitment and failing. But, if you do everything you're taught in the course, and you do it right, with the right people around you, you're halfway there."

Lloyd looks thoughtful. "Do you think the difference has to do with other people having had the power to decide whether to let you do the things you were trying to do, in contrast to doing development, where it was ultimately down to you to decide what you wanted to do? Certainly, the financial commitment and borrowing money from people is further motivation to finish a site."

"Accountability is unquestionably critical", Stuart admits. "One thing you'll often hear me say is: Why should anyone invest in you, if you're not willing to invest in yourself? That's why I chose to bite the bullet, and invested in myself with the one-day and three-day courses and the retreat in Bali.

"When you borrow money", Stuart continues, "from people you know to do the development... You talk about this in your book, the 'OSM' or '"Oh shit!" moment', where, while it feels good to have found the money you need to do the deal, you're now responsible to repay it." He smiles. "It's such a good feeling, though, when you've paid everyone back from the profits and there's some left there, at the end. You've done what you've been taught on the courses, and it's worked.

Now, you're ready to continue on, to move on to the next deal, the next deal, and the deal after that, and get bigger and better at development. I find that extremely exciting."

Andi leans forward. "We often remind everyone that the first development is the hardest, it's the biggest tackle, and requires a mindset shift that only you can make, yourself. Add to that the fact that if you have people around you who are perhaps a bit negative, you've got to work your way through that. And it's not necessarily that they don't believe in you, but, like you, they don't want you to fail. Most of us, like you, have tried and failed at things in the past. For you it was rugby, the Royal Marines, and the oil rigs, and perhaps they've been witness to that part of your journey. You can only move forward by taking that plunge, taking first step.

"For you", he adds, "you had to work out how to get funding, how to do your due diligence, how to get the offer to the vendor accepted – these are all things you've never faced before; it's the first time you've ever tackled this. But, as you continue to move forward, you break those challenges down into more manageable tasks. By the time you're tackling your second development, you've probably got a bank of investors, and you have a better feel for how to address the challenges that inevitably arise, because it's just that bit more familiar. And different people have different risk tolerances when investing and will ask a lot of questions, like, as you said, 'How are you doing this?' The learning curve in becoming a developer, like anything else significant, is very heavy at the front end. It's only the people who stick through it to the end who are successful. Over time, it tends to become easier, doesn't it?"

"It does, yes", Stuart says. "'Visibility is credibility', as you so often say. It's surprising even how many estate agents are aware of what we've done, and who come to us with similarly sized plots of land that aren't on the market yet, asking if we'd be interested. And I'm amazed by the number of people I know who are coming forward with money they'd stashed away, looking to invest. 'How much interest would you give us, if we decided to invest?', they ask. It is so true: Once you get that first development over the line, it's amazing what other doors open up."

"Have you any advice for anyone who might be listening to, or reading, this who are interested in property development?", Lloyd asks.

"The first thing I'd recommend is that they do what I did and get educated. It's not enough to just decide you want to take your life in a different direction. You need the tools, and you need to learn how to use them properly. And I'll say it right now, given my experience with training both before and after White Box, I would recommend they find a White Box training. As I said earlier, I've been on a couple of property courses in the past, although not all were on developments, but there was nothing I found that could hold a candle to what White Box deliver. I haven't seen you guys for a while now, not since Bali, but I feel like I've got a relationship with you both, knowing that I can always pick up the phone and ask you your opinion on something I'm grappling with.

"The proof is in the pudding", he adds, "and not just with me. Look at all of your students who have gone on to succeed in this. I would 100% recommend investing in this industry, and sourcing White Box. Even if you don't invest right now, do some research. And then commit to moving forward."

"We appreciate that", Lloyd says. "So, our final question:

What's next? I know you're looking at a few sites. Are you still employed? Are you still doing your job?"

"Yes, I'm still doing my job", Stuart admits. "If I hadn't had that debt from when I was younger that I needed to pay off, given that I'm self-employed, I could have probably relaxed a little bit more and maybe shifted to working just part-time while looking for the next site, which is Wakefield. But I had to pay that off as soon as I could.

"Now, though, the site we're looking at in York is a big one, with a potential £1.2 million profit, which is obviously is massive. If that goes ahead, I definitely will quit my regular job and go into property full-time, working on my sites rather than working elsewhere, where I've been forced to spend so much time away from my family."

"It's also reassuring for people who might be listening to, or reading this, to know that, as you've proven, you can get into this successfully, even if you are in some debt, that it's not that you need a stash of money first", Lloyd says. "You can succeed – and get out of debt – but it's only going to happen if you're willing to put the time and effort in. You, however, are proof that it can happen, if you're willing to do just that."

FRANK ARKO-THARKOR

http://www.tharkorgroup.com/

https://m.facebook.com/tharkorgroup

Instagram: @tharkorgroup

22-garage site, St James, Northampton

Here, we introduce you to Frank Akor-Tharkor. Frank is a qualified QS, a quantity surveyor. Now, we know what you might be thinking after learning that – that he came in knowing a lot about the residential property world. Well, as it happens, not loads, as he was not a QS for residential property. Instead, it was commercial, so although Frank has skills that do transfer to property, he needed to learn how to do property development first.

Frank attended our Property Developers Secrets course in January 2021 and was intrigued as to how one could become a developer. Frank is tenacious by nature and wanted to get started quickly, straight after the training, which is great. After a couple of false starts on some so-called interesting deals, he eventually started off with a simple conversion project. On this project though, he found his team, he found the process, and he found a few challenges along the way.

Frank has just secured another site and has many more now, in the pipeline, following his activity early on.

"Today", Lloyd says, "Frank Akor-Tharkor is joining us. Let's get into your story, Frank. You've come quite a long way since you did the White Box Property Developer Secrets course last

year, as you're very nearly finished with your first site now. We'll talk about that in just a moment, but, first, give us some general background. What are you doing now, and what is your background before getting into property developments?"

"I wear quite a few hats", Frank admits. "My 'day job', if you will, is working on a nuclear build as a quantity surveyor. I'm one of the senior commercial managers on that project. But I started my property development journey a couple of years ago.

"The thought has always been there, in the back of my mind, to get into some aspect of property. But it was only in late 2020 that I began to research, wondering, What do I need to do? Where do I start? How do I start? And that's when I chanced on the White Box PDS course.

"I began watching quite a few of your YouTube videos, which I thought were really good. Then, I bought your Property Development book, which was a great help, and while I was reading that, I said to my wife, 'This is the course that I really need to get on.' And so I did.

"The PDS course formulated in my mind what I needed to do to get into property. It was an eye opener. Obviously, coming from a construction background, I've always been sort of a major civil professional, but when I took the course, that's when it hit me: There's a lot to learn here! That was when I knew this would get me to where I am now."

"There is quite a difference between reading the book, which is a great intro, and actually taking the three-day course", Lloyd says. "For you, though, what was the catalyst, the thing that changed everything? By that I mean, what fell into place

when you read the book, and then when you did the course?"

Frank thinks for a moment.

"I suppose the golden thread within that book was the honesty that came across from you about the challenges involved. I've listened to quite a lot of YouTube recordings from other sources, and read quite a few other books on property, all of which made it sound as if it were all rosy – you get in there and make your millions, that sort of thing. But there was something that really stood out to me about your book, comparing it to others I'd read, and then seeing you guys on YouTube, the frank way you talk about the journey – I sensed an honesty there that I didn't feel with anyone else. It was very straightforward, pointing out all the risks as well as the gains. That's what spurred me to register for the PDS course. I wanted to make that investment to see what it really is like. If nothing else, I would be making an investment in my future. I know the value of education. I paid over £10,000 for my master's degree in construction management, so I felt the price of a three-day course was well worth it. And that was before I even knew about the Mastermind program. The idea was just to come on the course and educate myself, so I could get started on my property development journey."

"A lot of people talk about return on investment", Lloyd says, "so, yes, let's talk about your return on investment in your education. Having done our three-day course, what have you then gone on to do in development? What's currently in your pipeline?"

"I remember you guys talking about your first project, a garage, that you'd got from an auction. I came away from that PDS course thinking that, whatever my first deal turns out

to be, I've got a timeline now that I'm going to use to get my first deal done. So, I scoured all of the various land sourcing routes – Google, auctions, RightMove, etc. – and fortunately, within a few months, I landed on my first project, which was a garage, coincidentally, a workshop/garage which I bought off auction for about £120,000 or so. We took off from there, but it was not without its challenges."

"Where are you now with it?" Andi asks. "And what sorts of challenges?"

"Well, the garage had a planning in place to convert it into a two-bedroom detached house, so the plan when we bought it was to do just that. We had done the numbers, which seemed to stack up. As I said, we bought it off auction for £120,000. Having looked at the GDV within the area, £125,000 was the ceiling I'd set. And currently, we're scheduled to finish in one week. The painting and rendering are being done this week, and we've already sold it."

"What were you expecting in terms of profit?" Lloyd asks.

"About a 26% margin", Frank says.

"Impressive! It's just one build, one unit", says Lloyd, "which I think is quite a key thing to emphasise. A lot of people think, when they look at developments, that it has to be 10, 20, or 30 houses, whereas this was a conversion of a garage into one single unit. To generate a 26% profit on one unit is awesome, and a lot more than you invested in your property education. So, when we talk about the return on education, that is exactly what this is."

"Absolutely", Frank agrees. "That first deal more than covered that investment, but my focus on return was more long term.

I think most of the time people focus on the initial investment cost without necessarily thinking about the long term when, long term, the return on that education is unbelievably magnified. It really is unbelievable. I am a living example of that."

"So, let's talk about the challenges you faced in that development", Lloyd says. "Developments aren't easy. As we explain to people who take the course like you did, there will invariably be challenges along the way. One of your challenges we know quite well, in detail, because you're on the Mastermind program and we discussed it at length. Explain to our audience what you faced."

"We were quite excited when we first bought the property at auction. Obviously, once the hammer goes down, the deposit, the down payment, is deducted. I went out there, just being neighbourly, to talk to the neighbours and tell them that I'm a new property developer here, that I'd bought this property and was going to develop it. Just being friendly. So, when I was talking to one of the neighbours, they said, 'Do you know you can't actually develop this? There's a covenant on the land that says you can't actually develop it into residential.'

"Naturally, I was a bit confused, because we had planning approval to do just that. So, I went back and examined the auction document and saw that, just before the auction date, the documents had been updated to add the covenant, but the photocopy was very, very faint – you couldn't actually read it properly, so even if I had seen it, had reread all the documents right before the auction, I would not have realised what it was. It transpired that three other people had actually bought the property and returned it, back to auction, because they couldn't do anything with it.

"It was a nerve-wracking time, having invested my family's financial resources into this, only to hit such an obstacle. There was a Mastermind session scheduled just a few weeks after that, so I brought it up there and the group discussed it. Several suggested we try to get the neighbour to release the covenant. To cut a long story short, we had to pay to have the covenant released so we could proceed with the development, but it wasn't an easy process. What made a big difference, though, was being able to talk this through with the Mastermind members, as we could see a way forward that hadn't been visible to us initially. But it all rested with the neighbour, whether they were willing to release that covenant or not."

"I remember that day very clearly", Andi recalls, "and how we talked it all through. You joined that session by video, because you couldn't make the live session, and this was a big issue you were grappling with. There are people who've had that issue before who were unable to solve it and, instead, had to relist it on auction. And I remember you had a list of five or six different options on the whiteboard behind you, in your office, which you'd already identified yourself. The one which was getting them to release the covenant had been crossed out, because the neighbour had said very clearly the day you spoke that releasing it wasn't an option. So that was a dead end, as far as you were concerned. Three other people had tried it, he'd told you, and it wasn't going to happen. That's the benefit of talking it through with a group of your peers and mentors. We talked it out, discussed and empathised with the reasons they would be telling you that, and identified what the benefits would be to them, either way. And because we had done that, you were able to go back that that neighbour and present the situation in an entirely different way to how

the previous buyers had approached it, and demonstrate the benefits to him if he released the covenant. That's what enabled you to succeed when no one else had, wasn't it?"

"That's absolutely correct. The neighbour actually told me that my approach had been different from the three others who had approached him. He had been adamant that he wasn't going to sell or release that covenant, 'come what may', he'd said, that he wasn't even going to put a price on it. But by my talking him through all the strategies that we had discussed at the Mastermind, we were able to negotiate the release of the covenant."

Lloyd nods. "That's the power of the Mastermind, isn't it? Being able to talk through any challenges, examine all the different options, scenarios, and suggestions the members raise. So, yes, that was a great result in the end.

"You've had some other positives following this as well, haven't you?" Lloyd adds. "This isn't the only site you'll be discussing today, is it?" He chuckles. "We often liken it to the London bus, where you wait forever for one to come along and as soon as it does, there's another one right around the corner, behind it. But in your case, it's not two London buses – it's three or four now, isn't it? So, you certainly are motoring on and getting a few sites under your belt."

Frank smiles. "Absolutely. One of the things, and I give you credit for this one, repeating one of your favourite quotes, 'Activity creates opportunity', was about the buyback of this site which we were developing. Somebody saw it, and then saw one we had advertised on Rightmove, and as a result, he approached us about another project we might want to look into, one that hadn't yet been advertised on the market. We put in an offer, and we're still negotiating, because they changed the goalposts slightly. It was originally 10 semidetached units, but they've reduced it to nine units, yet they still want the same price as we offered for 10. That's a sticking point for us, so, we're still negotiating.

"But following that, we've got another offer accepted, this one on six dwellings, a mixture of a terrace and two semidetached, not too far from here. That wasn't on the market either. It was the result of a letter we had written to the owner, one of the procedures you suggest. They were just about to put it on the market, but called us and said, 'Let's see what we can do'. That just came in, over this past weekend. So we're really pleased with that. We still have some due diligence to complete on it before moving forward, but it's another example of activity creating opportunity. We're following through on what you teach and how you have laid all this stuff down – to write letters, for example – we have kept doing all that, which seems to be producing real results for us now."

"I remember in the early days", Andi interjects, "you were bringing things to the Mastermind, Frank. You had done the Property Developer Secrets three-day course, you took the information you got in the course to find opportunities and bring them to the table, and then you'd run them by us. It was quite a frustrating time for you initially, as you couldn't find anything that stacked in your area. You found a pub, didn't you, that you were looking to convert, put a lot of effort into that, did a lot of quotes for the build and all that kind of thing, but it just didn't quite stack up. That always feels disappointing, when you're trying to get started and nothing seems right, and you find yourself having to start yet again.

"But, in fact, it's all part of the learning process, isn't it",

he points out, "all the time. And then you got the garage conversion. Again, as you noted, activity creates opportunity. The first one's always the hardest to find, but after that it all opens up, doesn't it? You start to build confidence, build credibility, and now look at where you're at – you've got two or three other good-sized deals going now. It's absolutely brilliant."

"Absolutely", Frank agrees. "There will always be problems that you must face, always challenges along the way. One of my favourite quotes is from the motivational speaker Tony Robbins, who says that problems are only problems when you're going through them at the time. Once time passes, you look back on what seemed like a huge problem and realize that either it's become irrelevant or you've learned quite a bit from it. Right?

"My learning curve, the learning opportunities that I had when assessing the pub, all through the covenant release phase – all that has been invaluable. It's priceless, because I take it with me now, when assessing other projects, and make it pay for me, again and again. Honestly, if my first find had been straightforward and successful, I probably would have got lazy and assumed that was how everything would go all the time. If, from the moment I went on Rightmove, I saw my first land, assessed it, everything stacked up, and it provided 25% profit, so then I bought it, and everything went hunky dory, it wouldn't have taught me anything. But", he admits, "it's not pleasant when you're struggling to find that first site. Still, six months later, when I look back on it, I'm grateful for the challenges that I went through, because now it helps me to assess sites and makes it easier to have that conversation with vendors and clients, and even estate agents and such."

"Well, it sounds like you're doing really well", Lloyd says. "What would you say was the biggest fear you faced before you started? What's one thing you were thinking? Like, 'I just don't understand this' or 'I don't quite get that'. Anything that held you off from getting started earlier?"

"I suppose the biggest issue for me was money", Frank confesses. "I was concerned that I hadn't got enough money to start – only the little money we'd been able to save as a family. If I went and invested it into a property and it didn't go well, then where am I, you know? So, a big issue for me was available cash, and then, obviously, fear of the unknown. I didn't think that I was well and fully equipped in terms of knowledge to get started. But having been on the three-day White Box course and having gained some knowledge – and to be honest, I'm still learning, right? – but having gained some knowledge, I felt that the time was right.

"My wife is very risk averse", Frank says. "So, I had to do my due diligence to convince her that this was the right thing to do. Now she's fully on board, she understands what I'm doing, and gives me the support that I need to push these things forward. But I thought that lack of money was my problem, not necessarily the development itself. I felt I just needed a big load of cash to buy land and then do the development. It's true, though, that once you get the right land that stacks up, people are willing to fund the project."

"Do you still have those fears now about money?" Lloyd asks. "Or is that all in the past?"

"No, I don't worry about that now. I haven't got £500,000 to pay for the land we've just bought", he says, chuckling, "so it definitely isn't an issue anymore. It's about finding the land

that stacks up, and then speaking to potential investors who want to invest in that development."

"The challenges of each development are a gift, really", Lloyd says, "and it's the same with finding money. A lot of people starting out, or who want to start, think that they are at a disadvantage by not having enough money. If you had £500,000 in the bank, that seems like it'd be the easy route. You'd use your money and crack on. But if you think about it, in that event you'd always limit yourself to deals that you could afford on your own, whereas the best deals out there might be just out of your price range. You might not even know about them because you're limiting yourself to a certain cost ceiling. Moving beyond that limitation can be a real gift, though, because you must learn how to use other people's money. If you never learn how to use other people's money and give them the opportunity to invest it, you're just going to stay where you are."

Frank nods. "And giving people the chance to make a little money – it's a win–win thing, isn't it? You get to make a little money and others get to make a little money. Then, collectively, if everyone is bringing in a return of, say, £100,000, you can do so much more, because they're seeing good returns and they're willing to reinvest in you because they understand and have experienced your vision.

I think that's where the line is. Because if I had had the £500,000 to do it myself, the next time I would be putting only my own money into it, and so it becomes difficult to scale up. But scalability increases dramatically when the person, or persons, who have invested £100,000 might now have £200,000 and be willing to invest further. Therefore, scalability grows commensurately."

"And it only takes one deal to start", Lloyd notes. "So, tell us, Frank, if you had approached someone two years ago for advice on getting started, what advice would you have found valuable – something that would help someone else now who might be thinking about getting started?"

"To research", Frank says, without hesitation. "I would say it would be to research – a lot! Read a lot of books and get in the right frame of mind. You get what you put in. This is not a get-rich-quick scheme. Instead, you get out of it what you put in. The more effort you put in, the more return you get. The Bible says it too, that whatever you sow, that's what you reap. What you harvest is the direct result of what you sow, the effort that you put in, day and night, finding sites and such. And education is a part of that effort, that investment. You can't put a price on education."

"It's a case of actually doing something", Lloyd says. "You can't just become a successful developer simply because you decide it's what you want to do. You have to put some effort into becoming one, to take the necessary steps to do it. First comes making the choice, which you did. You chose to read my book, and you chose to research other sources as well. You did the three-day course after that, and then, from there, you chose to act, to put what you'd learned into practice.

"That said", he adds, "a lot of people undertake learning, but fear and doubt prevents them from taking the next step and actually putting what they've learned into practice. They've got to make that choice to change their mind. You've got to believe."

"That's true", Frank says. "When I took the PDS course, I met quite a few people and made quite a few friends. Some of

them have yet to dip their toe in the water, though. But they've sent me messages, saying, 'We're watching your progress. You're doing well, Frank.'

"And I say to them, 'So, what's preventing you from making a start?' They've been on the same course, the same course we've taken together, but they haven't progressed as much. So, doing the course isn't the be all and end all. You have to take the next step and actually do something. If you don't put your education in motion, then what value does it really have?"

"As they say, 'You can lead a horse to water, but you can't make him drink'", Lloyd notes. "We'll take you to the water's edge, but you've got to decide to drink.

"Well, we're looking forward to continuing to follow you and help you along, and hear all about this new site you've got. I'm sure there'll be a few challenges with it, and we're always here to help you through them. It's been great to witness your journey so far, to see the ups and the downs, because whenever there is a down, it's great to see the upside afterwards."

"Thank you, both", Frank says. "You guys have been amazingly generous with the support you've provided me. I'm particularly grateful for the Mastermind program and how much it's helped me."

MIKE & CAREY MCKEOWN – MATRIX DEVELOPMENTS

http://www.matrix-developments.co.uk/

http://www.matrixconsultancygroup.co.uk/

http://rentmyhouse.co.uk/

Instagram - @matrixconsultgp

Mike and Carey McKeown are a husband-and-wife duo from Hereford. They came to White Box Property Solutions Ltd. with a background in the property industry, having owned a few buy-to-let properties, and had been concentrating on serviced accommodation business, renting houses out on a nightly basis on sites like Airbnb. They first met Andi Cooke on a serviced accommodation Mastermind, because at that time, we, at White Box, had converted four houses and three pubs into 82 serviced accommodation units that we were running. As we were not experts at that strategy, we were investing in some education, as anyone should, to learn from people who are experienced in doing the same.

Mike and Carey also owned a letting agency at that time, managing other people's investment properties, and had been doing so for eight years when they met Andi. Their intention had never been to build out sites as they are doing now; instead they merely intended to build a single house on a plot next to a property they already owned. However, after talking to Andi, their mindset and intention soon changed.

This is how their podcast episode went.

"Thank you for having us", Mike says, as he and Carey take their seats. "As you know, we've been a part of the White Box community for about three years now, and we've done the Property Developers Secrets course, the PDS, several times. Since we began learning from White Box, we've assembled a small team, began putting everything we've learned into practice, and started building houses. We're currently in construction on our second site, after the first one was such a huge success, and it's all thanks to you guys. Our first site gave us the traction we needed, and we now have the momentum and pipeline to continue to develop and put what we've learned into action – profitable action."

"That's great!" Andi exclaims. "Now, when we first met, it was at a training course for something else you're both into: serviced accommodation. And you had your own letting agency. Where would you say developments were in your vision at that point, in 2018?"

"At that point, nowhere", Carey admits. "As you noted, we met in a serviced accommodation boardroom, back when Mike and I had a letting agency. We ran that business for eight years and then sold it, without ever giving much thought to the property development side of things. But I think it was the natural follow-on for us from running the letting agency.

"We've always had buy-to-let properties, being a landlord, as you can imagine. We became really interested in the property development side of things", she adds, "after initially speaking with Andi, when we had a buy-to-let with a potential plot next door. We also wondered if we should buy the house and then sell the plot next to it. When we spoke with Andi, he suggested we'd be better off selling the plot after getting planning permission. So, we took his advice and put the money we made into our first development."

Lloyd nods. "Mike, you mentioned that your first sell was a massive success. That's a big statement. Can you explain in more detail what that first deal was? Carey, you said you saw the plot of land and you ultimately chose to do a bigger site, something that you didn't think you could do straight away, until we all discussed what would be involved in doing a bigger deal. So, would you explain that first deal for our listeners: the figures, the number of houses, and how it all worked out?"

Mike leans forward slightly. "Well, we had considered trying to build the initial one plot out. But Andi explained to us the economies of scale in terms of building multiples at the same time and how it would be relatively comparable, in terms of the work needed and the costs, to build multiple houses versus building a single plot. In fact, that's something you guys brought up during the training session."

"At first, we tested the water", he says, glancing at Carey, "by attending White Box's Discovery Day. That was enough to convince us, right then and there, to invest in the three-day Property Developers Secrets course. And that's where we met you, Lloyd, and were able to discuss our specific options with you to build out a bigger site. That said, the first time we did the three-day course, I was still focused on our serviced accommodation business."

Mike later confessed that when he initially attended the course, he took in the information but admitted that he was too busy running the day-to-day operations of his serviced accommodation business to do anything with the knowledge, despite also attending our Property Developers Mastermind Monthly. It wasn't until he attended the course a second time, now accompanied by his youngest son, that the magnitude of what we were talking about, and what he could build, registered.

"So, yeah, we decided to come back and do the course a second time", Mike says, "during which I had a lightbulb moment. That's when I realised how much information there was to take on that first time around. It was only after that reinforcement, after absorbing the information more comprehensively that second time, that it really sank in, what you guys were saying about building a team. It dawned on me that I could build a team, with me like a football manager. And that I had a fairly good idea as to where I could source the skills we'd need. After all, I was already in the property industry, although in a different aspect of it. But I knew some builders, I knew really good architects. I also knew that I could access the necessary funding through our service accommodation links. It was like I'd shaken all the pieces to the jigsaw out of the box, and now I just needed to put them together correctly.

"So, then we spent about 18 months trying to find a site that 'stacked', a combination from a pipeline of sites without planning that potentially could work. But", he adds, "after chatting with you at our monthly Mastermind sessions, we started to look at sites that already had planning approval, because you had advised that a site with planning provided the path of least resistance in terms of getting a development under our belt.

"With that in mind, we found a site that had failed at auction. I think we just lucked out and came along at the right time, as the agent was about to lose the instruction after they'd put it to auction and it failed, and they were about to lose it to a competitor. We contacted the agent and they arranged with the vendor to let us take it on, outside of auction. The site had planning in place for three detached houses – two four-beds and a three-bed – but executive-size houses, a really good size.

"The site was a little tight, but we felt we could make it work because it's in a really good area", Mike says. "It's got good transport links to the M50 and the M5, and it's about 14 minutes from where we live. That meant the build costs would be the same as the first project we'd had in mind, but the end values would be much higher. From there, we put the team together, got everybody to have a look at it, and funded the purchase of the site ourselves, having kept in mind what you advised us about things being easier if the site was unencumbered.

"We initially estimated the GDV (gross development value) slightly lower at first", Mike says. "We calculated that it would be about £1.2 million. And Covid-19 as well as other factors complicated things over the course of the build. But housing prices were creeping up, which obviously worked in our favour. Our team of four comprises two builders, an architect, and me handling business administration, the admin side of things. Our guys were building at a cost of only about £108–110 per square foot, considerably lower than had we brought in a main contractor, and that allowed us to create a really good product. We were planning to price them at an average of about £495,000 – specifically, £525,000, £495,000, and £475,000. It turned out, though, that we sold one of the two four-beds for £550,000 and the three-bed for £500,000, and we decided to keep the remaining four-bed, which had a value of roughly £550,000 by then. That enabled us to pull out £200,000 profit from two sales and pay off all the finance. Between that and the last one we kept, the profit was about

£412,000. But if we'd sold the remaining four-bed for that same £550,000 price we got for the first, our profit would have been about £730,000."

Lloyd shakes his head in admiration. "That is indeed incredible for your first-ever deal, in terms of developments. Your first new-build project was only three houses – three houses. That is a big deal for most people. I realise you've seen people in our monthly Mastermind group doing bigger sites, but for three houses to generate a potential £730,000 profit, assuming you'd sold that third site, is insanely successful! Most people would hear that and think it's too good to be true, or that you've been doing this for many years, and that it's a level you've built up to, instead of just off the starting block."

Lloyd grins. "But it isn't too good to be true –that's not the case – and this is precisely what this book is about. It's to highlight the stories, the realities of people who have done these deals, people who are in the process of doing a deal, and some who are just starting out, so that others can see how attainable success is in this industry if you have the right mindset and belief from the start."

Developments are profitable, as a rule. And there is a stigma that people outside the industry place on developers, thinking they're all greedy and in it just for the money. But that isn't the case. As developers, we have to jump through a lot of hoops: we have to wade through significant compliance requirements, make innumerable on-the-spot decisions, we risk our family homes in some instances when we use them for collateral against the money we borrow, all to build homes for other people.

Mike and Carey had the passion for property before they got

started. They participated in the Property Developers Secret course more than once, because they had the desire to do something, but they only realised the £730,000 profit from the deal once they chose to make it their priority. Mike admitted that he spent 18 months scouting around for development possibilities, but he wasn't fully dedicating his time to it because he was running another business.

However, once he and Carey changed their mindset and prioritised doing developments, everything fell into place. This highlights the pivotal difference between someone who dips a toe into the pool with the idea of testing the waters and someone who commits to diving in to developments and makes a success of it.

"Obviously, that £730,000 is split between you and your investors", Lloyd points out, "but that's a plenty big pot for everyone". He looks at Carey. "What would you say your biggest fear was before doing the deal? As we noted earlier, you had some experience in property already, which is a good start, but what would you say was your biggest fear in terms of getting into development, a specific area of property that was new for you?"

Carey considers the question for a moment. "Well, we had different fears, really. My biggest fear, especially while we were taking the three-day course, was: How are we ever going to fund this? I knew Mike and I would never be able to fully fund it ourselves. The idea of having to ask people for money – it felt like we were poor and asking our family for money to support us! But once I took a deep breath and spoke to family and friends, I gained a new perspective on what it was that we were looking to do. I realised that in a way, in a very distinct way, we were offering them an opportunity to do more with their money than letting it sit, passively, at the bank, earning next to nothing. The interest rates were – and still are – so low at the moment that people we knew had started to pull all their money out of things like premium bonds and savings accounts, where they were getting virtually nothing in return."

Lloyd nods. "That's a great point to stress, to review, because a lot of people will relate to this part about the hesitation, the mindset towards finding the funds to do their projects. It feels like scrounging money from family and friends to do a development. People don't want to ask friends and family, because they don't want to be seen as begging for assistance. But while it might feel to you like you're begging for money, for help, it's not at all what you're doing. What you're doing is offering people you care about the chance to make an investment at a far higher rate of return than they'd ever get from a bank. Your investment vehicle, which are developments, enables the people who are important to you to earn more for their money. So, you're not asking them to help you, per se, and you only. You're banding together – you're helping each other. That change in perspective is something people like yourselves need to have in order for your entire team to succeed."

Carey smiles. "It was a massive mindset block for me at first. Initially, I admit I hesitated, thinking I could never tackle that part of it."

"I think I'm a little bit more laid back", Mike says, looking at Carey, who's nodding. "My fear was probably more about my credibility, that when I spoke to friends and family, their reaction would be along the lines of: What's this latest scheme that Mike's got now? Right.

"In fairness", Mike admits, "it may have been a little easier for us to approach people, because we could demonstrate that we'd already run a profitable business, had sold it on, and we'd done well with that. But this was still, admittedly, new territory, somewhat of an unknown, and so I think my primary fear was messing it up, selling the dream to people I care about, investing their money, and unintentionally messing it up somehow. Admittedly though, we weren't trying to do this in isolation, just winging it, because we had built this team of two experienced builders and an architect. We weren't novices. We also had White Box to lean on for advice and reap the benefits of your experience and successful track record."

"Agreed", Andi says. "When it comes to building a team around you, we always say it's like being the conductor of an orchestra. You don't have to be able to play every instrument; you just have to be someone who can guide everyone to work together, to get each orchestra member to play their instrument at the right time, in sync, in order to create something others will appreciate.

"Your power team, as we call it – you're the architect of that. You sourced the builders, the guys who built that plot of land, the one you later sold, through your network, through your personal contact with them. I think you told us that you played football with them on a Wednesday night, or something. And that the architect was someone you played darts with.

"So, your power team comprises people who were already around you in a nonprofessional environment", Andi continues. "These are people who possessed the knowledge and experience to do that deal on their own. But what was lacking was someone to bring it all together, to orchestrate it. And that someone was you."

Mike nods in agreement. "Without a doubt. You were right that it's about identifying people I already knew, people in different walks of life, and bringing them together to leverage their skills and experience. There are probably a lot of people like me who could do the same thing, but they just haven't considered it. They're not aware of the possibilities available to them."

"What's also important to note", Andi says, "is what this experience has done for your power team members who were already professionals. This was, I'm guessing, a bigger deal than any they might have worked on in the past; plus, it was more profitable – they got more money doing this development with you than they would have, had they simply continued working as a contractor." Andi leans back in his chair with a grin. "What was their reaction to the outcome?"

Mike shakes his head. "It was unquestionably a radical undertaking for them. Before this, they thought of themselves as occupying a one-off role, that their job was to construct a single building and then move on to the next job, the next project, all for the exclusive benefit of someone else. The whole letting side of things – keeping the property as an asset, and having it produce ongoing cash flow in their own pockets – was definitely a radical concept. But they're over the moon with it. At the moment, we're building eight houses on a site, and everything is working that much more smoothly – it seems that much easier than it was before, even though it's nearly three times the number of houses. The more we do, the easier it becomes, which is not something I would have originally thought would be the case. I just assumed larger projects would be more complicated. I think that's come as a surprise to all of us."

"I think it's a massive point to make", Carey interjects, "how important the relationship between everybody is. Mike is, like you said, orchestrating it all, and my job is to nurture and maintain that relationship. It can be delicate. For example, we've got money still tied up in this last house, the four-bed from the first development, and two out of the four of our power team are a bit anxious to realise the money. Or sometimes the builders demand more and more from the architect, who's snowed under, and Mike's perpetually ironing out these wrinkles. Behind the scenes, below the calm surface that others see, there's literally so much going on.

"This is why I obviously like being able to network with you guys, because you know exactly what's involved. You've had plenty of experiencing managing all those relationships, and you sometimes are having to do it at a distance."

Lloyd nods as Andi says, "Definitely. You mentioned earlier that you're finding it easier now, because you've since done more houses, but it's also easier because you've been through a deal and your team have seen the results. The builders see that you completed that first project, sold some of it, and you've got some cash flow now. So, now they can go into the next one with confidence, knowing that the process works and that they just need to focus on their end, the build end of things."

"Without a doubt. Initially, during the first project, we may all have been keeping an eye on things like cash flow, worrying about the job as a whole, but now our team members can focus, undistracted, on their own bits and pieces, confident that things are working and they don't have to be concerned. Everyone's fully committed now, because they've seen the process works."

Lloyd nods. "You mentioned that you're working on your next site now. If I remember right, it's been about three years since you first started with us, but things didn't move forward for about 18 months, because you weren't wholly dedicated – you had your other business to manage. You said that your decision to retake the PDS course, the Property Developers Secrets course, to reinvigorate you is what motivated you to move forward in a more purposeful manner, and that's when you found your first development site."

Mike reflects, "I probably wasted half of that 18 months because we were still heavily involved in setting up our service accommodation business. I'd glance at the calendar and think, 'Oh, God, I'm going to the White Box PDS course in a couple of days', but I'd only give it a minimum amount of attention. I think you'd agree that some of the proposed sites I brought made it evident that not a lot of thought had gone into the process. It was always a bit of a rush to pull together a few possibilities."

"No, I didn't really notice that, Mike", Andi drawls, teasingly.

Laughter

"You mean when you brought those 10 crap sites for John and I to look at. Yeah."

More laughter.

Mike exchanges a grin with Carey. "So, you can imagine", he says to Andi and Lloyd, chuckling, "having stood on that stage last weekend during the awards ceremony, there's no way any of us would have imagined ourselves having done all that three years ago!"

"You're currently, at the time this recording is being done and this book is being written", Lloyd clarifies for the audience, "White Box's Developers of the Year for 2021. And you're only three years into this! That is incredible. But out of everyone we taught in 2021, and there have been a lot of success stories, you two – the deals you've been doing and your commitment to what you've done – were the obvious choice to win that award.

"Give credit to yourself", Lloyd insists, "for doing that. Despite not being focused in the first nine months or more, where you were interested but it wasn't yet your priority, once you took the PDS course again, it catalysed you into giving it your all. What's really to your credit is that you did dive in, you committed fully, and didn't give up. A lot of people would have given up after six months, making the excuse that they're not ready for it, that they've got no time to dedicate to it.

"You didn't", Lloyd continues. "Instead of waiting to find the time, you made the time. Imagine! If you had given up instead of seeing it through, you wouldn't have realised that £730,000 first deal. And you wouldn't have this second deal you're working on now. Let's talk about that second deal. Let's talk about how that came about. And if anyone's wants to see this site you're working on, and the previous one, head over to our White Box Property Solutions YouTube channel. We've got a video of Mike on his site on our channel, guiding viewers through the first finished development, and Andi touring it and sharing the details of how it came about.

"But let's talk about the second site", he says. "How did that come about? Would you share with us the figures, and the current status?"

Mike leans forward in his chair. "Right now, we're building eight houses on a site we picked up that already had planning in place. We'd gone to have a look at it during the build of our first project.

"What we learned fairly quickly is that a lot of these deals take weeks, months, even years sometimes to get over the line. I didn't want to be in a situation where we finished the first project without having anything else lined up to continue on with. So, we've always maintained a pipeline of sites that are either in planning or in legals, and those are our potentials. Meanwhile, we've got other sites we pick up that come with planning. We paid half a million pounds for this second site that came with full planning for eight houses: five three-beds, one four-bed, and two two-beds, a much bigger project than our first one.

"So, in calculating the initial GDV," Mike explains, "the gross development value, of that second site, our projected profit was about £700,000. Now that we're well into it, everything just seems to be working so much more easily. We've got things lined up in advance, because of how much we learned from our first site.

"There's also been a shift in the market", Mike adds. "The profit on that now looks like it's going to double, from our original estimate of £700,000 to about £1.3–1.4 million.

"That one came about, if you can believe it", he chuckles, "because the wife of one of our builders alerted us to a site near where they live that she'd driven past, and so we arranged a viewing with the agent.

"This is quite key to what you guys teach", Mike says. "So, we went to have a look. It was on for £550,000. Carey, myself, and the architect analysed the figures and decided we could probably make it work at half a million. We offered that and it was accepted. Meanwhile, the builders looked at each other and asked, 'Uh, how are we going to pay for that?' 'Don't worry about that', we said." Mike chuckles. "We literally did it like that: we offered, right then and there, on the site after we'd viewed it and we got it all put into legals, all the while having no idea as to how we were going to pay for it.

"But I just knew from experience that by following the process, leveraging the contacts we already had, and the fact that we were already doing a site, that we had demonstrated that we could do this. This time, one of our rental-house clients came on board, supporting us with a percentage of the initial land purchase, while Carey and I and the other directors put in the rest. He's over the moon, as well. He loves that he got in on this."

Andi chuckles. "One of my favourite sayings, as you probably know, is: 'Activity creates opportunity'. The first site, that's the activity in this equation – you've done that – and keeping that pipeline going and trusting the process has generated strong relationships with your existing investors, and that created opportunity for you, leading you to your next site. You just trusted the process and it manifested accordingly. That's just brilliant."

"And as we mention in the YouTube video", Mike adds, "back when we talked about where we were with regard to Redmarley, our first site, we were in legals then, for the adjoining field. Since that video, we've come away from Redmarley, finished that development, and gone on to the second one, which is near to Shropshire. During that time, we wrote to the landowner of the adjoining field in Redmarley inquiring whether he was interested in selling, agreed to a deal that's since gone through legals, and we've been granted planning permission on it now. That's due to start at the end of January 2022, so it will overlap the existing site project near Shropshire. That is new territory for us too, where we'll have two sites on the go at the same time. And the third site, the vacant lot next to ours, that's what I'd call a classic White Box procedure: we identified the site as a potential whilst working on the current site, we sent them a directive and a letter, and it's now firmly in our pipeline."

"What are the figures on that one?" Andi asks.

"It's quite similar to the one that's underway", Mike replies. "We've got planning for nine houses, but two dwellings have to be provided as affordable housing, because it's classed as a rural development. Those two are two one-bedroom flats and a two-bedroom house, which leaves us with six dwellings and an anticipated profit between £850,000 and £1 million. Actually, I'm being conservative with that, as it's probably likely to go over the £1 million pounds, given that it's such a good area. Again, good location, easy access to transport, plus the housing market's working in our favour at the moment."

Lloyd leans back in his chair with a smile. "Again, imagine if you'd given up after six months!"

Laughter.

"This is why", Mike says, "when I speak to people in the White Box network who are a few years behind where we are now, who recently joined us, I like to tell them that if we can do it..."

"I think what's always been good, though, for you guys, and especially you, Mike", Andi says, "is that you've always thrown yourself into everything that White Box offers: the fitness groups, the white collar boxing we were doing before the first lockdown... Anything you hear about that we're doing. You trust the White Box community so much – you just get involved, it's as simple as that.

Mike nods, smiling slightly. "That's me getting myself out of my comfort zone. I'm quite shy, and even when I do stuff like write student social media posts on the White Box community's WhatsApp group, I tend to be a bit hesitant; I don't often post in these forums as often as I should. Even talking here, now, like when you, Lloyd, asked me about the profit we made from our first deal, I find myself hesitating, like, well, first of all, I'm aware that it almost doesn't sound believable. But what I've learned, and what I do often share when talking to others, is how important it is to get out of one's comfort zone and commit to these projects fully. That's the only way it's going to succeed. It's why I think we've benefited so much, so quickly." He glances at Carey.

"I agree", she says. "And keeping the pipeline flowing is important, which is one of the things we've learned from our time with White Box. Some of what's percolating now stems from actions we took early on, even as far back as the beginning of our journey. We've had three or four people respond to letters we'd written to them months or even a few years earlier. They all say, 'Oh, you wrote to me a while back. I'm thinking of selling my land now. Do you want to meet?'"

She shakes her head. "It's funny how it can be such a struggle in the beginning and then all of a sudden – like you always say – it pays off. I mean, I sold our dining table the other week on

Facebook to a guy. And outside our house is a plaque Mike's brother bought us years and years ago – we've been there 14 years – and it says 'McKeown Towers'. So, this guy who's buying the table shows up, sees the plaque, and says, 'This isn't Mike McKeown's house, is it? He works with Ben James, the architect?' I couldn't believe it when he said that Mike and Ben had written to him a while back about selling his land. 'I'm still interested, if they want to get in touch', he said. And this happened because I was just selling a table!" She shakes her head in a mixture of delight and disbelief.

Mike glances at her. "You know, I just spoke to that guy yesterday. Ben and I have got a meeting with him at the end of January."

"Brilliant!" Lloyd exclaims. "Now, you mentioned something about the help that we provide. You've been with us, what, three years now? What would you say has been the best part of that? For example, how did we help you get started?"

Mike thinks for a moment. "So many different ways, really. I think [the White Box retreat in] Bali was pretty special for us, as well as the classes and overall support. For anyone who's considering the White Box retreats, I would certainly recommend them. It was good in unexpected ways, ways that are sort of hard to put into a sentence or two. Everybody says that, when they're at any of these retreats, it's difficult to convey just what's involved, what you're going to get from it. You can't grasp it until you're actually there, until you experience it for yourself.

"For me, I often find myself referring back to the notes that we made on the discussions, the vision shared, thinking about things we wouldn't normally think about when we're busy with the day-to-day stuff – the renewed focus on our goals, thinking about where we're going and where we want to be, which we might otherwise not have given much, if any, real consideration to. That was one of the valuable things we've gained. But it's more than that. The community now, it's massive, and I think we've got friends for life that we've met through White Box, whether it was at the retreat or in the monthly Mastermind sessions – like-minded individuals. That's just so important, isn't it?"

"I totally agree", Carey says. "When I think back to the three-day Property Developers Secrets course, which I only did once, I remember sitting there and thinking just how much there was to take in. When you covered the building side of things, I thought, well, I don't know how to build a house. But what I could take on board were things like the direct vendor letters and the money side of things. That's where my contribution would lie. And that goes back to the White Box advice about putting together a team. You can't possibly do everything yourself – you've got to build a complementary team around you first, like we have. Mike and I may have won that White Box Developer of the Year award last week, but we couldn't have done it without our team. Each team member comes with their own distinct experience and skillsets. We all have our different strengths. Mike does the project management side of things, Ben, our architect, manages the design, and the builders handle the construction end of things. What's important to remember for anyone starting out is that you can't do it all yourself. Surround yourself with people who can do what you can't, and you'll be just fine."

Lloyd nods. "Yes, and for us, it's not just about teaching you how to become developers; it's about teaching you how to build your dream team, your power team. But while we can teach you how, we can't do it for you. It's you who have to go out there and do it. When it comes to developments, every site is different – no two sites are identical. But it's a very bespoke kind of training, the sort of advice we give, which is tailored to each situation. But while we deliver the message, it's you who have delivered the product, having taken the White Box message on board. The proof is there – you've done it, you're still doing it, and it's been nothing short of impressive.

"It's also the overall mindset of things", Mike says. "Some months when I'm joining Andi's Mastermind group, I'm not going in with anything I need to discuss in terms of the practical, build-side of things, but there might be something more on the personal side of things, a changing relationship, for example. And I really appreciate that I have that avenue, that the format isn't regimented but, instead, is tailored, as you said, to each person's needs at that moment. That's really valuable."

"A lot of it is about vision", Andi observes. "You have to believe it to achieve it. We can paint the broader picture for the White Box community, the people. But you, Carey and Mike, you are inspiring so many people who are following you, because they can see your first day, and it's tangible, they can see the profit you've made, they could probably even go and look around the site, if they chose to, or look at it on YouTube. It shows them definitively how the process works, that it will work if they follow it and commit to it."

"That's a good point", Mike says, "because when we stood on that stage last week, I wish I'd said more about the previous winners whom we've always looked up to, who inspired and helped us, because that's really important. Like Sonny, Kevin, and Craig. We used to lean on Kevin and Craig a lot, because of the types of projects they were doing. Our dream was to be as successful as they are. The same could be said for Matt and Ian – they were really helpful. So, I agree that by inspiring others, and proving that the process works, it enables us to be there for those people in the community coming up behind us in much the same way."

Lloyd looks at Carey. "So, for anyone who's on the fence about getting into property, what sort of advice would you give them?"

"I'd say what I've said to several people over the last few years: You have got to be prepared to take a risk and not overanalyse. We've seen a number of people go through the Mastermind who like to analyse sites, but over-analyse them to the point where they talk themselves out of it." She looks at Mike. "For example, with your first site, you took the risk, without ever imagining that it was going to generate the profit that it did."

Mike nods. "I think that if you're someone who's very intellectual, you can sometimes be your own worst enemy, if you know what I mean, because individuals like that can analyse data to an extent far beyond what I'd ever be able to do", he says, and adds with a chuckle, "and I would never want to. I don't mean to sound like I'm a little bit reckless, but Carey's right, you can spend too long detailing some things until you talk yourself right out of it. As you guys have said to us in the past, at some point you've got to get some plates spinning, haven't you?

"We've learned so much from our first development project that we're more confident now in our ability to have a few plates spinning rather than just one. That's a place we never would have got to, had we not decided to move forward with the first one."

"You can't make a profit without putting an offer in", points out Lloyd. "You've got to be prepared to follow through with your education and put what you've learned into practice. There's not much point investing time and money into learning something if you're not going to put it into action afterwards. Putting what you learned into practice is precisely what you've done, and the proof is there, for everyone to see."

"And it just keeps getting better and better", Mike says. "For example, the site that we're on now has an adjoining field, so, we're in legals with that as well, so we'll no doubt be darting back and forth between Herefordshire and Shropshire, doing bits and pieces. One just seems to lead to the next, and to the next", he says with a grin. "In fact, just last week we were invited to view a plot off-market, which we think will quite comfortably accommodate about 30 houses. That lead came through one of our power team members, a builder who did some plastering for the lady who owns it. She knows now, from him, that he's building his own houses, and she likes him so much that she wants us to have it!"

"Not bad for a shy couple who weren't in development three years ago", Andi jokes.

Laughter.

"Your story is really inspiring for people", Andi says. "It's so good for people who are in that first six to nine months, struggling to find a site that stacks, to be reminded to just keep moving forward, to keep with the process, that you were once in that same boat – we all were! It really does bear repeating how funny it is, as you say, that once you get one under your belt, they start flowing to you more effortlessly, that it really does open up the pipeline."

"To the point", Mike says, "where just yesterday we instructed a commercial agent on one of our sites, because we think we've almost got too much. We're thinking about maybe selling one, to not try and build them all, that maybe that's the sensible thing to do at this moment."

Lloyd nods. "That is sensible. While it's important to try, you can't take too much on at once, as much as people would love to do as many sites as possible. Sometimes, it's just not that possible. It's a great thing to be open to your options, to sell some, work on others, and have a different strategy for each one." Lloyd leans back in his chair and asks, "If you could summarise White Box in a word, or a sentence or two, how would you describe White Box?"

Mike doesn't hesitate. "Genuine is the word that comes to mind. Unfortunately, there are training providers out there who don't deliver. It's a bit like mechanics – you get one rogue mechanic and then, all of a sudden, you think all mechanics are rogues. One bad apple. I think it's a similar sort of thing in the property world, from a training aspect. But that's not White Box. The proof is in the pudding. You guys are just genuine. I say that because some trainers only focus on their successes and avoid discussing their failures to where it comes across as unrealistic, a little too rosy. You, on the other hand, disclose the good and bad that you've experienced on your journeys, because you want everyone in the community to benefit from your experience, to learn how to tackle failure. It's not all going to work out ideally, effortlessly. You teach us how to cope with that, to overcome it. So, yeah, I definitely think 'genuine' is how to describe White Box." He looks at Carey.

"Definitely", she says, nodding.

Lloyd smiles. "Well, thank you both very much. So, if any of our listeners or readers want to follow Mike and Carey McKeown's journey, head over to the social media handles, follow them, and see what they're doing." He grins. "And if anyone knows of any sites in Shropshire and Herefordshire areas, you know who to contact! Thanks again."

DARREN BROGDEN - BRYTR HOMES

Instagram - @brytrhomes

In this chapter we talk to Darren Brogden, who, at the time of writing this, has just opened the doors to his recently converted pub into a wine bar, something that Darren is passionate about, on the ground floor of a commercial-to-residential conversion he's done. Darren used to drink in that very pub just a few years ago, and now he's converted it. It just goes to show that you never know where your next deal might come from.

We first met Darren on our Property Developers Discovery Day, in 2021. Darren was looking for a career change, as he felt his job was under threat after the pandemic hit. Darren was an airline pilot for cargo, yet he always had an interest in property. Stemming from the information we shared with him on Discovery Day, Darren joined White Box's three-day course, and we have been helping him ever since. We've even shared the odd red wine with him from time to time!

"Today we're talking to Darren Brogden", Andi says. "It's really good to have you join us. Now, to start, you did well at our 2021 End-of-Year Awards."

Darren smiles. "It was a great party. You all did a great job organizing that. Yes, I was surprised and pleased to have won two awards, one for Newcomer of the Year, with this first year having been a terrific intro to what you at White Box are doing in developments, and the second for Conversion Deal of the Year, projects I've got going on in Wantage that are set to take off next week."

"Our Newcomer of the Year award", Lloyd explains, "is for those who have made strong progress within just six months of starting. That's quite a short amount of time, given what's involved, for someone new to make solid advancements in property development. What were you doing before getting into property developments?"

"Aviation, actually. I've got 30 years in aviation – 11 years in the Air Force flying DC-10s, and then the last 20 years flying 747s, mostly in and out of Hong Kong. So, when COVID-19 came along, it had a big impact on what I was doing. I'd already been contemplating pivoting out of aviation at some point, but COVID was a major catalyst. By late 2020, the industry was feeling the effects. And while I was considering my options, I came across Lloyd's book, Property Development, the secrets to becoming a property developer. It sounded like a solid strategy, that you and Andi had been successful in what you were doing, and I was intrigued by the fact that you were teaching this, you were leading students and people in my position to develop their own projects. Curious, I attended the White Box introductory course, liked what I heard and saw, and that convinced me to do the three-day course, so much so that, straight away, I signed up for a mentor program, which was a big step. That and the discussion I had with my wife when I got home!"

Laughter.

"And it's all been absolutely brilliant", Darren says. "What you guys at White Box do, in terms of what you give to students and what I've got from it, is really incredible, I have to say. That's where my progress has been. My approach before I took your courses and read the book was a bit scattergun. I didn't really know what I was doing. So, the fact that you've been able to structure and strengthen my focus has been superb. I feel much more confident now, in terms of understanding what I need to do and what I need to be looking at. The fact that there's a lot of help and support available to me, both at White Box and from everybody in the Mastermind group, has made all the difference."

"Well, what you've accomplished in such a short amount of time is impressive", Lloyd says. "The one thread that links everyone we interview on this podcast is that the education they've received has contributed enormously to the success they've each achieved. You had the interest, you had the desire, you had the passion to do property, but you weren't sure what was the best way to begin. It's not enough to just say, Hey, I'd like to do property!, as every developer takes on different types of projects. So, we try to go beyond just providing the basics, the common threads, and additionally offer support and expertise for all sorts of projects, small and large. Having that knowledge, that education, helps you better focus on precisely what it is you would like to tackle.

"What's great about you", he adds, "is that you listen and take on board everything bit of information and advice we provide. You follow it, step by step, and every month, when you join the group, we give you as assignment of sorts, like ask you to do some bid, you go off and do it, and you return the next month, say, 'Okay, I've done this. What do I do now?' That's how to get results. Most of the success of our students derives from being willing to follow the next step in front of them, and to not overthink it, not psych yourself out about doing it."

"Well, I think it's important in all aspects of life to actually learn from people who have hands-on experience, who know what they're talking about. If someone thinks they can do better without that", Darren says, chuckling, "good luck to them, but, generally, I think most of us learn best by following successful people and taking their advice."

"Your previous career", Lloyd points out, "personifies that. There's no way you would ever have been able to fly those planes without proper training beforehand. If you had just jumped in a plane with a load of passengers seated behind you and only then thought, Okay, how do I do this?, there'd be chaos, there'd be carnage. You wouldn't get behind the wheel of a car either, without learning both how to do it and the rules of the road, right? It's the same with development. A lot of people jump into it impulsively, without sufficient knowledge, preparation, or even the most basic understanding of what's involved. And that generates chaos."

Darren nods. "And it's not as if you learn the basics and start doing and stop learning. Throughout my 30-year career piloting airplanes, I never stopped learning. There are always situations you encounter that are new to you, that you learn from. All industries change, best practices change, at least to a certain extent, and the same can be said for building and developing. Every development will be unique in its own way, and you're going to learn new things as you go – new ways to tackle problems, new materials available to you, keeping up on changes in regulations, and so on.

"You might have six different people look at the same simple plot or building", he says, "and end up with half a dozen different ideas on what could be done with it. There's no single way to approach every project. It's an ongoing educational, evolutionary process."

"One of the things I wrote in my first book", Lloyd says, "was about using us, at White Box, as mentors. A mentor is a bit like an air traffic controller, which you, Darren, can certainly relate to, overseeing and guiding you on your journey, to help ensure you end up in the right place. It's a good analogy, I think, and it's important in your development journey from A to B, to anticipate and be prepared for potential turbulence along on the way. Having someone there to help guide you in your journey is a huge benefit. Forewarned is forearmed, if you will.

"So", he adds, "let's pilot this conversation towards the deal you're looking at, at the moment. What are you working on right now?"

"The most imminent project is a pub conversion", Darren says. "It's a Grade 2 listed building, just over 200 years old, with a pub on the ground floor and some existing residential accommodation above it. We've got permission to change the upper floors into individual apartments, and while there's no planning permission to change the pub itself, we've got permission to change a kitchen annex into accommodation.

"There have been a few challenges along the way", he admits, chuckling. "Another type of planning permission was refused, which led to us having to renegotiate the whole deal. Fortunately, we've arguably got a better deal now, with an opportunity to come back to the planning commission in the future.

"So, the main task", he continues, "is a rather extensive refurbishment, primarily to tackle acute acoustic mitigation measures, so that any noise emanating from the pub doesn't intrude on the residential accommodation upstairs. The remainder is merely reconfiguring, rewiring, and redecorating. It's quite an interesting project. Lots of issues have arisen in just the last couple of weeks that have introduced potential delays, but most of that has more to do with my inexperience than anything else. It's just a massive learning process, all the time." He grins. "I have to admit that I rather enjoy when challenges arise, because I'm learning more and I enjoy figuring out ways to mitigate whatever problem has come up. Luckily", he adds, laughing, "I've got an old mate of mine who's in the building trade, and he's going to be keeping an eye on most of the bills for me.

"I'm really enjoying this phase of it", he adds, "putting the deal together, making sure we've got the architect working with the builder... With all the utilities that are coming in – electrics, plumbing, etc. – it's a constant challenge, a bit of a jigsaw puzzle, if you will, but I'm really enjoying identifying the pieces and fitting them where they need to be.

"We complete the deal next week, go straight into the strip-out, and then we'll go from there. I'm sure we'll uncover quite a few more challenges in the next week or two", he adds, chuckling.

"So, you could say, in a way, that you're the conductor of the orchestra", Andi says. "We tell people right through the training that they don't have to do everything themselves. If building is not your thing, you can get someone in to do the building. But someone – you, the developer – has to orchestrate things and put the deal together. You don't have to play the instruments; you just have to put in place someone who can."

"That's true", Darren says. "When you begin, you're dealing with the agents who do their bit and maybe they make you aware of things you weren't previously aware of. Then the solicitor steps in to provide their particular expertise. Then you add the architect, who tells you about things in that realm that you need to think about, things you might not been aware of but that you need to consider. The orchestra conductor is a good analogy, I think, working with different musicians and pulling them all together. It's important to remember that you don't know what you don't know, and to listen to all of these expert 'musicians' who are advising you on what it is they do in order to create a great outcome."

"And we have mentors as part of the group", Andi says. "So, if you're not sure about something, you can take it to the group and see if someone else has overcome a similar challenge, and how, and they can then guide you along the way."

"Absolutely. I personally found the group a massive help", Darren says. "There's so much knowledge within it, and a willingness – a desire – to help everybody with any problems they're having. It is a really friendly, helpful group of people; plus, it's inspirational to learn what fellow developers are doing."

Lloyd nods. "The benefits of the White Box community are substantial. Surrounding yourself with people doing the very thing that you're looking to do is a positive thing. If you surround yourself with people who don't understand what you're doing, why you're doing it, or who don't know how to do what you're doing, that's not terribly helpful, is it? Sometimes, people don't appreciate or understand the value of having such a large community around you, why you'd need or want to be in a room loaded with people doing the same thing essentially, but you've embraced it and credit some of your success to it. You've, in fact, done a joint venture or two with several people in the Mastermind group, haven't you? You're doing some amazing deals.

"So, on the pub conversion", he continues, "what is the profit you estimate making?"

"Well, it did change from the initial plan, admittedly. We were denied the extra planning permission we sought, losing out on about £200,000 of profit from that, which is why we ended up having to renegotiate the deal with the vendor. I'd estimate that the adjusted GDV, the gross development value, is now just £650,000, but that's without assessing any value to the pub.

"That was a challenge, actually, because lenders don't really want to lend on pubs at the moment, given the COVID-19 environment, so it's difficult to value reliably. The good news is that we've already lined up a tenant who's going to take over that part of the build and do a lot of the fitting out himself, thereby reducing our costs. That's because he's going to turn it into a wine bar, which I think is quite exciting.

"So, we know what rental income that will generate, and with the yield on that, we estimate a value of about £250,000 on that. So that brings the property's GDV up to about £850,000–900,000, depending on how you work it out.

"We've got total costs somewhere around £600,000, so we're forecasting a good £300,000–350,000 profit. That's before we uncover all the other problems that we haven't accounted for", he adds, laughing.

Lloyd grins. "Now, tell us, given your experience in both, what do you prefer: flying or property?"

"That's like asking me to choose my favourite child, isn't it?" He laughs and shakes his head. "No, I'm not going to do that! I had a fantastic career flying airplanes and loved so many aspects of it, but for a while now I'd been thinking that it was time for a change, and this has turned out to be a brilliant opportunity. I absolutely love the challenge of what's ahead. Obviously, it's all new and exciting still, and I'm just itching to really get into development. I had a great aviation career, no question, but I'm really excited about what's next."

"I remember", Andi notes, "on that original Discovery Day about six months or so ago, you struck me as a sensible guy. You needed proof that this concept that White Box was putting forth was solid. You were understandably cautious versus just impulsively diving in. You wanted first to see that there was some substance to what we were presenting. Looking back now, given how well you've done, you must be pretty pleased."

"Yes, I'm delighted with the way it's gone", Darren admits. "There was understandably a certain amount of trepidation in stepping away from aviation altogether. A lot of my colleagues who have gone through redundancy recently have found other aviation-related jobs, so that would have been a nice, easy safety net to fall into. I really wanted a new challenge though. I wanted to push myself, to prove to myself that I could do something else, that I wasn't just a one-trick pony", he adds, chuckling. "I wanted to test getting into a new career, but I knew that in order for me to really fully embrace that, to totally commit to it, I had to make a clean break from aviation, which would force me to make this second career a success."

Lloyd nods. "Tell us, what would you say your biggest fear was about getting into property, before the initial education part? And has that fear been alleviated since you introduced yourself to White Box and the community?"

"The unknown, I suppose", Darren admits. "And the fear hasn't gone away entirely, but that's not a bad thing. Fear can be good. It means you're acknowledging that you're not someone who thinks they know it all. You're not going to relax and be too casual about it. You need a driver, a catalyst, some impetus to keep you focused and moving forward. There's a lot of trepidation about the future, of course there is, but that's not the point. The point is that I've got a solid community around me that offers support. I've got a good partner on my team who knows what he's doing, and we work very well together. I've got you guys at White Box, the support group. And there's an exciting energy to the fact that I'm learning all the time. So, yes, there is a level of trepidation, of course, which is natural. Having been a commercial pilot for so many years, I'm used to being careful and not taking unnecessary risks. So, while there's a risk involved with this, I feel comfortable knowing that I've got the support I need around me."

"One of the things we emphasize at White Box", Lloyd notes, "is that no one does developments in isolation. Sure, you'll have various team members and contractors doing particular tasks, so it can be deceptively easy to convince yourself that you can do this yourself, with just that small team around you. A lot of people try to shoulder that on their own. But developments are easier and more successful – and less frightening when problems arise, which, more often than not, they do! – if you have a support group with people who are more knowledgeable and experienced than you.

"So, if you're a builder, and your project requires a build, our advice is not to try and do it wholly on your own. And even if you're not intending to do it yourself, when it comes to developments, you're actually better off being in a management capacity, to be free to focus on the bigger picture rather than trying to be onsite, tools in hand, doing it yourself. I think you've gauged that very well. You've got the skills to source the people that you need to do what they're good at. I think that has been one of the keys to your success."

"Well, that's definitely my plan. I'm definitely not going to be handling the tools. My DIY skills are pretty average", Darren says, chuckling. "My plan is to let people do what they're good at, whether it's a bricklayer, electrician, carpenter, whatever. The key is to get the experts in, let them do what they're good at, and meanwhile I'll do what I'm better at, which is managing people and orchestrating the entire process."

"Can you describe for us what your future plans are, what your long-term vision is?" Lloyd asks.

"Well, I'm really still at the starting block here", Darren admits. "Right now, I want to focus on this one and see how we do, and hopefully we'll make a profit – I'm pretty sure we will. Then we've got a second project lined up, and right now I'm tentatively defining the pipeline beyond that. For example, in the joint venture project we've got, we've been approaching the neighbours on either side of that floor. We've had a nibble, but nothing concrete yet. Between that and following up on the other leads that are coming in all the time... Well, it's about simple strategies, like you say, both in your book and on your course, about talking to people, putting ideas out there. It's amazing what people can bring to you when you share with them that you're getting into property developing, and you're looking for possible projects, for options and sites. I found it surprising how many people I know who suddenly shared that they were involved in their own little projects, or looking at a piece of land, or that a friend of theirs has something. It's all networking. You just have to have that conversation. Admittedly, many of the ideas proposed to me won't eventuate into anything, but one or even some of them will. It's amazing, now that I've put it out there what I'm doing, how many opportunities are coming my way."

"Activity creates opportunity", Lloyd says. "Somebody said that, but no idea who."

Andi adds, "Yes, it's about telling everyone what you do. And even if you hesitate, because maybe you feel that imposter syndrome that we all feel when we start something new, you've got to embrace it, you've got to talk to people about what you're doing. There will always be people who are looking to invest money, some who might even surprise you. Or they might have a land opportunity for you. Everybody's pipeline is populated by looking within their own world. If you want to be successful, you have to speak to everyone you know, no matter how unlikely they might seem. That's how opportunities come to you."

"For anyone who is thinking about exploring or getting into developing", Lloyd asks, "what advice would you give?"

"First off, based on my own experience, I'd say to go and take the White Box course. It's a small investment that will not just help you make a go of it but also to be really sure that it suits you and that you're suited to it, that you really are willing to commit to it. You're not going to know if this is really a good fit for you until you actually educate yourself as to what's involved, to find out all of what doing development involves. That was my first step, the Property Developers Secrets course that White Box offers, after I'd read the Property Development book. That really brought into focus everything this involves and how I could make a success of it. I had to do that course, before anything else, in order to best analyse whether I could make this work, whether I wanted to make it work, whether I was truly prepared to take that next step and commit to it wholly. And after that, it's really up to you, you've got to take that risk, to ready yourself to take that plunge. You've got to have confidence that you can do it. You guys at White Box work hard to instil that self-confidence in your course, and boost it with your support network, but, ultimately, you, yourself, have got to be prepared to take the risks required.

"In fact, if there's one thing that I really took away from the PDS course, it was the motivational portion. White Box incorporates a lot of that, and it was the Will Smith video that really resonated with me, the one where he's parachuting in Dubai and he says, 'The best things in life are built on the other side of fear'. That resonated with me because I knew I had to get over any fear I had about taking the next steps. It's all too easy, too comfortable, to sit with what you know and remain in your rather confining comfort zone. If I had done that, avoided the fear that comes with trying anything new, I'd have continued in the aviation field. But I knew that if I wanted to succeed, then I had to get over that fear of leaving the comfortable environment that I've known for 30 years and take that step forward in a new direction.

"I think that the first step is getting educated", he adds. "Find a solid resource or two, like I did with White Box's courses and book, and find out from those who are in the know just what lies ahead and how to tackle it. Then take the second step, take that leap, like I did. Based on my education and experience so far, I don't think I'm going to regret having done this."

Lloyd nods. "The education is the how. You had identified the what, which was what you thought you wanted to do, after reading the book and taking the intro and PDS courses. You had the why, because redundancy was looming and you weren't sure you wanted to continue in another type of aviation job but instead try something different, stepping out of that comfort zone you mentioned, instead of just taking an easy, more familiar path. If you want personal growth, as the experts say, you have to put yourself in an environment that isn't familiar, which is precisely what you did. So, hats off to you! Your commitment and willingness to take that risk is why you were awarded Newcomer of the Year.

"The deal you're currently doing, the commercial conversion deal, is a great deal too" Lloyd says. "You actually found that on the market, didn't you? It wasn't a word-of-mouth referral situation."

"That's right", Darren says. "I don't know how long it had been on the market for, but there was a lot about it that, for me, was quite serendipitous. One, it just looked like a good deal. And it was in the town where my business partner lives, so that was an excellent hook to get him involved. We'd had conversations about doing a deal together somewhere, but he was hemming and hawing, and then I showed him this and said, 'How about this deal? It's literally around the corner.' It's also about just 30 yards from where my wife, Heidi, and I bought our first house together. In fact, I remember going into that pub 20 years ago", he adds, laughing, "and thinking it was a bit crap back then."

"Things do happen for a reason", Lloyd agrees.

"We'll bring some life back into it", Darren says, "and I think we're going to do a pretty good job, especially with the tenant we've got lined up for the pub space. He's really excited about turning this into a wine bar and is prepared to invest quite a bit in its redesign. So, all round, it's looking very promising."

"If anyone is interested in following your journey", Lloyd asks, "where can they find you?"

"Well, I'll be putting quite a bit on LinkedIn to document some of the progress on the project and keep everyone up to date. I might post some updates on Facebook for those who know me there, but the primary place would be LinkedIn."

"Excellent", Lloyd says. "Thanks very much, Darren."

MATT BAKER - SCOTT BAKER PROPERTIES

Insta/LI/FB: @clearlymattbaker

Insta/LI/FB: @TheHMOPlatform

Insta/LI/FB: @scottbakerproperties

Matt Baker was on our very first Property Developers Mastermind, one of our very first White Box courses, and he has attended many of our Business and Personal Development Retreats in Bali, Croatia, and Monaco over the years. He is a great friend to White Box and has done many things in his business built on our support. His business partner Niall has also become a very good friend of White Box and, together, they continue to achieve great things.

"Today, we've got Matt Baker with us", Andi says. "Welcome to the podcast. You've been with us for a while now, but you were pretty new to developments when you started with us. Would you tell us a bit about your journey thus far?"

"Well, I started in property investing back in 2015", Matt says, "with a semidetached bungalow, a very small refurbishment, and that got me eager to tackle something juicier. I did a couple of HMO developments, and it was in 2016, amidst the third HMO development, when I met you, when we bought the old office of Insurance House. That was our first major conversion project, where we converted it into an eight-bed HMO and one-bed flats.

"Since then, we've done a few different types of projects. We had an offer accepted on a piece of land, got planning on it, and then flipped it. I did an interview with Lloyd for the White

Box YouTube channel, so anyone can find that video where we discussed that particular project, because it was pretty painful, but I learned a lot from it.

"Since then, the focus has been on creating really high-quality HMOs – 'Next-Level HMOs', as we call them – and co-living properties. We've been doing that for about five years, ranging from houses to HMOs, and then offices and retail shops, using post-development rights and planning permissions to achieve really good-quality shared accommodation."

"You've been on a quite a varied journey there", Andi notes. "It's been probably five, six, or even seven years of challenges that have taken you to that point. And I know, myself, that each one of those has got its own story.

"Let's go back to the start of that", Andi suggests. "When we first met you, you'd done a couple of HMOs and were looking to get into bigger developments. You joined, I think, the third course we ever did, a two-day course that Neil Briggs, whom we've also interviewed, participated in, at the Hilton Hotel. The courses have increased in length to three days, as there's a lot more content now. There were a lot of people in the first couple of courses – as well as Neil Briggs there was Ricky Darlow, I remember – lots of people who took the course and have been smashing it in developments ever since.

"You also joined our Mastermind program for a while, where you discussed the project you just mentioned was so painful. You'd got a plot of land relatively quickly, but it ended up being quite a long journey, didn't it?"

"It did", Matt says, "and I sometimes ask myself whether I would do it again, although the answer is probably yes, because it was a really good deal on the face of it. It was a plot of land, one we came across quite by accident, when we were in an auctioneer's office, talking about some other properties. At the very end, we casually asked, 'Do you have anything else that might be of interest?' and he said yes, that they had some land they were trying to get into the auction, but the vendors had been taking a while to pull the information together.

"It had a valuation of about £430,000, he said, but they didn't think it was worth more than maybe £230,000. So, I said, 'If you can get us that valuation of £430,000, we'll see what we can do'. Well, he walked over to the bin and pulled out the valuation, which he'd ripped up and tossed, and showed it to us. And, later, he sent us a proper copy. So, we could then appraise it for the true market value which, I think, turned out to be £235,000, when we had a valuation of £430,000. We got what was essentially 100% bridging finance on it and bought it with that bridge. In fact, because we got a percentage of the value, and not a percentage of the purchase price, we were able to borrow about six months' worth of interest as well, up front. We put zero cash in it, apart from a little bit for the legals. Literally, a no-money-down deal."

"People are always asking if it's possible to do a deal without money", Andi points out, "because it seems impossible to do it without money. Typically, there's got to be some injection of money at the start with development – it's pretty rare that you can get lending to cover all of the land price and all of the build. But in this instance, because even though you had agreed on a lower purchase price, the amount you were lent was based on the £430,000 valuation, which you had on paper from the valuer."

"That's correct", Matt says. "We paid £235,000, but we

got 70% financing based on the £430,000 value, so about £300,000, minus the fees. And it came with planning permission for 21 flats. That said, we wanted to improve the planning permission, because those original flats that were agreed were really pokey, 21 flats over five storeys, originally, and we thought we could push it up to six storeys and get 22 flats out of it. The idea was to make each flat bigger, thereby more valuable, and go up an extra storey.

"So, we put it into planning, went back and forth with the planners, then got a recommendation for approval, only to be pulled into committee, where we got absolutely slated by the planning committee for reasons which were patently untrue. They bordered on almost personally slandering me and my parents – we were there, buying it together. It was really frustrating, because they refused it for reasons which were incorrect, inaccurate.

"We appealed, and anyone who has been in planning knows that an appeal can take six to nine months. Not including the time it had taken to get it into committee in the first place, it took about another seven or eight months to appeal, and all that time the clock was ticking on the bridge loan! What appeared to be relatively straightforward – quick in, get planning, go to development, finance – had left us, instead, stuck on this bridge. Then we lost the appeal! Not for the reasons the committee had cited, but for a different reason; I can't remember what it was now. I just remember looking at it with the architect and discovering that the inspector had made a mistake – he'd measured something wrong. And the only way to correct that mistake was to take it to High Court, and there was no point in doing that.

"Ultimately, what we did was resubmit the scheme, fixing

the issues, and finally got it through two years after we'd first bought it. So, we were on a bridge for two years trying to get the planning on it. And, essentially, we got exactly the same permission on it as we had asked for on day one, with only one very minor adjustment!

"So, yes, it was a long and winding road, which cost us quite a bit of money. By the end of that time, which was our first experience of planning, our first experience with committee, our first development, we were tired of it. We wanted to get rid of the land and recoup as much money as we could. I think we walked away with a £15,000 loss or thereabouts, a relatively cheap lesson to have learned. On a positive note, I spoke to the committee just this week, in fact it's the second time we've gone into committee, and so it's 50:50 so far in terms of experience."

Andi nods. "One really positive thing that people will hear about the start of your development journey is that you've had one that was dragged out, you lost a bit of money, but not much, given all the costs you incurred over those two years, your bridge interest, any private investor interest. To be just £15,000 down after that lengthy delay is, in hindsight, more a bit of a wash versus a major loss.

"Now, I'm going to be careful how I say this", Andi warns, "because I don't want people to jump into deals where it doesn't work, obviously, but your first experience was a bit unusual. Typically, people get into a deal and might spend two or three months, only to have their offer get pulled or something like that, and it doesn't actually happen. But it's better to have it happen that quickly, rather than what happened to you. You learn so much by getting in there and just doing it, going through the due diligence, going through the process, versus someone who is scared to pull the trigger because they're worried something will go wrong. It's a great learning experience."

"Definitely", Matt agrees. "I'm always glad that we learned what we did on one of our first deals, because if it had gone absolutely swimmingly the first time, we would probably have made a bigger mistake on a subsequent project. Instead, our experience made us cautious, maybe sometimes overly cautious on certain things, moving forward, but that's not necessarily a bad thing. We know, with clarity, what we're willing to do, and what we're not willing to do."

"Fair enough", Andi concurs. "It was quite a tight site, too, like a high street, and small frontage. Six floors up, and as I recall, high land at the back, and low land at the front..."

"A retaining wall on the main road on one side, a brewery on the other", Matt adds.

"Quite a difficult, pokey little building. I want to be sure our audience comes away from this not thinking that going in front of planning is automatically going to be a terrible experience. This particular site had a lot of things to overcome, specifically."

"Yes, it was a very awkward site for a first one, but we thought we'd give it a go. My dad had links to the site, so we were in a fairly good position to do it, had it gone easier in the beginning, without all the planning headaches."

"Let's look at what the rest of your journey has been then", Andi says. "After that, you decided that your bread and butter would be HMOs. That's what you had been doing, wasn't it, before you first took our course. You were good at getting angel investors, you were good at lining up the money, and good at finding sites. Tell us about that part of your journey and where are you now, with that?"

"Well, it really did focus us, because one thing we always knew we wanted was a high cash flow in properties – we wanted to retain as much as possible. The only thing we've ever sold is that land in Stockport; everything else we've bought, we've held.

"We've worked with probably over £2 million pounds' worth of investor finance over six or seven years, ranging from friends and family all the way through to a wider network that we've grown, with some amazing investors in the business. But when it comes to getting high cash flow from a smaller number of units in properties, HMOs are the best way to go, if you make sure that you get HMOs right. You've got to future-proof them, and the way you do that is by creating what we call Next-Level HMOs, which are a lot more resilient and provide great cash flow.

"The rule of thumb that we use", Matt adds, "is that we aim for the top 5% of the market when we create these properties. So, whichever market you go in, you can either create a new top 5% by basically blowing the competition out of the water, or by just going in and making your products, your house, your service different to that of everyone else.

"That's what we focus on, and also what we teach. Because, if you recall, a few years ago, when we went to a White Box retreat, you suggested, 'Why don't you share this information?' So, I did. I wrote a book, Next Level Landlord, and now we have a training platform called The HMO Platform."

"How many White Box retreats have you done now?" Andi asks.

I think I've done all except one", Matt says. "I've done all of the Bali retreats."

"We started those in 2017", Andi notes. "Three in Bali, a couple in Croatia, and one in Monaco, and you've been to virtually all of those, right? I remember when we said to you that the business retreat isn't just about property, that it's about any kind of business, and that we could help you with the training side of things." Andi smiles. "You set yourself a lofty goal at your first retreat, in 2017, as I recall, to get 100 rooms over the next 12 months. And you managed that by cycling through, getting bigger HMOs, and you found one of them on that retreat with John McDermott, didn't you?"

"I found two on that retreat", Matt says.

"And then we set you the goal to write your Next Level Landlord book", Andi says, "taking readers through your journey to develop Next-Level HMOs and how you became a next-level landlord. Tell us how that all came about."

"The goal to write a book was always there", Matt confesses. "I always knew I wanted to have a go at it. So, I started writing, and wrote about 60,000 words, at which point it made me re-focus and refine the strategy, how we do things, and put it into a succinct methodology. That improved the way that we coached and trained others, and also made me scrutinise how we were doing things and how we could do things better.

"Putting my ideas down, in writing, really helped, and then I worked with the publisher, Rethink Press, who released it, we got to number one on Amazon after the initial launch in

March 2021, and we've since revised it into a second edition, due out in March 2022."

"And when we post this interview", Andi says, "we'll post your details so people can find you, can contact you, and get your book, Next Level Landlord, as well. It's great, by the way. I got several copies at the original launch. Lloyd had just written his book when you made the plan to write yours, so he was able to help you through the process and help set up the formatting.

"The great lesson here", Andi adds, "is that we've discussed one of your so-called failures, the Stockport deal. But, of course, it wasn't a failure, because we only fail when we stop moving forward. Your five-, six-, seven-year story, though, is that you've got so many wins; you've now got the training platform, and you've got a Mastermind program for HMOs, which is very much like the Mastermind that we do for development. It's all been a challenge, but a good one, to get to where you are, hasn't it? When you started the HMO Mastermind, it was likely a challenge to fill one room, but now your program spans several days, doesn't it?"

Matt nods. "Yes. We've just started doing a third day, and we've just created a new product for the members who have been with us for a while, who really want to continue moving forward with us. The target is four days a month, during which we focus on coaching them on the deals they're doing. Since the end of 2019, our clients have done about £17 million in HMO-style deals, something we're very proud of."

"That really is impressive", Andi says. "What about you, yourself? What kind of deals are you working through at the moment?"

"Mainly commercial conversions", Matt says. "For example, one is a shopfront we bought in Portsmouth, a double-fronted shop that we managed to buy at £370,000, where you'd typically get a house only half that size for that price – so, essentially, double the amount of space for the same money. We're going into planning now to convert it to a 16-bed co-living space. And given our experience, and my experience with the Portsmouth city council committee, where one of the councillors stood up and basically said, 'This is exactly the type of HMO we want in Portsmouth', and their having slated HMOs for the entire three hours of that committee meeting, we'll likely end up back in committee with this one. I will be singing the praises of what we're doing and can showcase that it's yet another next level of HMOs. Even though it's 16 beds, it's a Next-Level HMO."

"You had that experience from the first committee, which didn't go well, did it?" Andi asks. "We often learn more when we have to struggle the first time than were we to dive in and have it go seamlessly. When it's seamless the first time round, only to then run up against a challenging committee, it might feel like an even greater struggle. But you've been very successful over the last few years, and you're an excellent example of a member of the White Box community, as you've been there, right from the start, and have done so many of our retreats. You even came to Lloyd's 30th birthday!"

"That was a great night!" Matt says, grinning.

"These retreats are really inclusive", Andi adds, "and with the nights out, as well. We're all a big family really, and we've just started up another level, business boardrooms, and you've joined that too, become part of an even more extended community. Tell us: How do you feel about that side of it?"

"Very happy, and excited to get into it", Matt says. "We've always had coaches in some form since the beginning. I got into property because I did a training course, and White Box came along after that, looking at developments, probably a year after I did my first course. I took your course and became even more successful.

"I've had a different coach on building a business, not just the property business, which went well, but now we're growing, going back into developments, and because White Box runs training, and you are developers, and also you guys do letting, and we've got a management agency now, it makes sense for us to continue with the business boardroom side of it. Also, since the pandemic, we haven't really had a coach at the level that we want – people who are doing the types of developments that we want to move into, working at the level we want to be at. So being exposed more to those people in the group is going to be exciting."

"What would you suggest", Andi asks, "to someone who's looking at getting into developments or simply into property? What would your advice be on how they should start out?"

"I think the number one thing is to get the right people around you, first and foremost. That might sound convenient, because we do training, but it's what worked for us when we were starting, ourselves. It's certainly how you and Lloyd got started. Success isn't an accident. It's having the right people around you, to support you.

"My next piece of advice is not to go too big on the first one, to do something of a more manageable scale that still stretches you. I know that a lot of people talk about taking the 10x approach, but even just 3x or 5x, a bit more in your comfort zone, is better, as long as you've got the right people around you. Get those under your belt first, before becoming a bit too ambitious initially.

"For example, the path I set for myself was to just buy a little bungalow to start with, then do an HMO, then do a commercial conversion, then buy a plot of land. It's not like I would do 10 buy-to-lets and then go on to HMOs. I wanted it to progress quite quickly. Now, some people think that approach might be too risky, but I think, fundamentally, you can stretch it yourself. Just ensure you have the right support around you first."

"That's great advice", Andi says, nodding. "I know that you do what we do: we practice what we preach. If we find someone who wants to do HMOs, we refer them to you, because we want them to be trained by experienced professionals who can mitigate as much risk as possible for them."

"When we did service accommodation, we didn't know anything about it beforehand, so before we did anything, we found someone who taught service accommodation, went on their training, their mastermind, and got our team up to speed first."

"It's common sense really, to educate yourself before jumping in, to speak to someone who's done it before, someone who's aware of the pitfalls, who have learned the lessons. You've heard us talk about the lessons that we've learned. I know the lessons that you've learned, lessons you likely don't talk about on a day-to-day basis but that come out in these courses. We learn more every day, and that's why I love sharing that information with our clients, because they can take what we've learned and approach their projects differently, as a result." Matt chuckles. "Actually, quite often, they're even more successful and at a faster pace than we were, which is brilliant!"

Andi grins. "Definitely. We've had some of our Masterminders of the Year and Developers of the Year just smashing it! I'd say that our Developer of the Year, every year, is absolutely smashing it, and, like you say, probably progressing faster than we have. It makes sense, really, because they have us to steer them away from making all the mistakes that we made, so they benefit from a kind of compound growth of our knowledge, which is great."

"I agree", says Matt. "Their success is our success, at the end of the day. It showcases that the process really works."

MICK BARKER & ANNABEL BREWER – BE POSITIVE HOMES

Insta: @annabelbrewerproperty

Linked in: Annabel Brewer

FB: Annabel Brewer

Mick and Annabel are a superb duo. They met while networking and have teamed up to boost each other's skills. Mick has been involved in the development industry for years, watching other people succeed, and had wondered how he might do the same, but he never took the first move until he joined our Land Sourcing Academy. Following Lloyd's guidance, and employing his processes, Mick found a plot of land through an existing contact, just as Lloyd had suggested – simply by asking. From that moment on, Mick's thinking changed. He stopped hesitating and, instead, forged ahead into developments, feeling supported and confident. Here, he shares his story.

"Today", Lloyd begins, "we are joined by Annabel Brewer and Mick Barker".

"Good see you both again", Andi says. "We've been following your exciting journey over the past few months. You've come a long way since we first met you."

"Very exciting, isn't it? We've nearly completed our first venture together now", Annabel says, and Mick nods.

"We're finishing off a property that we bought as a joint venture", Mick explains, "a pair of large, semi-detached four-bedroom houses, about 1,600 square feet each. Everything's gone to plan, and we're plastering now. I was just informed that the kitchens arrived an hour ago on-site, the electricians have done their job, the plumbers have done their job. I drove to the site the other day and couldn't even get in through the front. There were 12 vans there, every trade you could think of – the site was absolutely buzzing. I looked at all the activity and was struck by the thought that this was all due to us, that Annabel and I were the reason for all of the work being done in front of me, and how we had created this work, this employment, for all of these craftsmen."

"It's a busy road it's on, too", Lloyd notes. "I remember, because we came and recorded for the White Box "Building the Dream" series on YouTube. So, tell us", Lloyd says, shifting the focus slightly, "in terms of figures, what do you estimate you're looking at for the end value?"

"It's £295,000 per house", Mick says, "so a total gross development value of £590,000. That was the price we'd originally set, what we were asking, and what we got. The person who bought the houses didn't even attempt to negotiate. They came in with asking, offering £295,000 each. I should note", he adds, "that next door there are four more houses, two other pairs of semi-detached houses that were built exactly the same, but with different materials used on the exterior. I mention this because I've been in the industry for 20 or 30 years with a building supply business, a brick and stone business, and I like to think that I can design a nice house, materials-wise. I imported our bricks from a factory in Holland, and I have to say that I think our houses look a hell of a lot better than those ones that have already been built. They look like housing estate-type homes, with bright orange roof tiles and thought given to creating an old, weathered look. Ours feature the old, weathered-looking ones with a bit of black weathering, a bit old-world looking, so the curb appeal's a lot better. They asked for £285,000 for theirs, the agent said, and they accepted lower offers on all of them. I don't think they achieved £285,000 on any of the four, whereas we got asking, £295,000 apiece. So, we were able to ask for, and get, an additional £10,000 per house, plus whatever differential they lost by selling below asking. And that was just because of the materials, the fact that we were thoughtful about the way they would look. And we're talking about no more than six months between when they sold theirs and we sold ours, so not enough of a time gap to attribute it to rising property values."

Andi nods. "A big fear for a lot of people looking to develop their own sites is: 'I'm not going to be able to rent them', or 'I'm not going to be able to sell them' at the end. You clearly felt very comfortable in your ability to plan everything and sell them off-plan. To get the plaster and other work done subsequently. It's reassuring to know that you can do that, that the market is there to sell them off-plan like that, isn't it?"

"I think it comes down to location, doesn't it, Mick?" Annabel suggests. "Mick lives just outside of York, which we all know is a highly desirable area to live. This particular village is about 25 minutes out of York, and is on the commuter belt, so we knew there would be demand for these houses on that basis alone, despite their being on a busy road.

"Thankfully", she adds, "we sourced excellent agents to sell these properties. They made it very clear to anyone who was inquiring that they are on a noisy, busy road. If the interested party was okay with that, then great – then they'd go and have a look at it, so nobody was wasting anyone else's time. We only had people who were very serious about buying and knew about the road. It really reinforced just how important it is to have a really hot agent, one who knows exactly what they're doing and knows the area inside and out."

"I agree", says Mick. "The road was an important factor, not just in terms of selling the finished properties but also back when it came to the initial value of the land when we were looking to buy. It had been on the market for quite a while, a year or two. Because I'm in the trade, I mentioned it to a number of builders who come in to buy bricks from me, but some had said, 'Oh, the land's too near the road; you'll never sell houses there'. But as I drove down it, I passed one, two, three, 10, 20, 100 houses and more on that same busy road and wondered why people would say no one would buy there if people were already living in all of those houses? Obviously, it would have an impact on the price – we'd have to discount for that – but if we factored that into our GDV, the gross development value, along with the build costs and the land value, what's not to like, I asked myself.

"So, I bought the site for £135,000 with planning for one big five-bedroom house. I knew no one would pay £500,000 or more for a single, large house on that roadside when, for the same money, they could be off the road, in a cul de sac, or whatever. But getting £295,000 each for two was feasible. And it worked."

"We talk about this at White Box a lot", Lloyd says, "how, when a lot of people interested in development talk to other people, what they hear is negative: 'Oh, you can't build that there', or 'That won't work', and they believe it, without questioning it first. You didn't. You listened to the negative and chose to investigate it yourself to see whether you thought it was correct. And it wasn't, was it? You thought through the process, instead of just abandoning it right then and there."

"The White Box message is very clear", Annabel says: 'Aim for the mass market, the vanilla houses.' So, that's what we did. We went for 4-bed family houses, nothing terribly high spec, because that location doesn't require it, and the council affirmed that those type of houses were in great demand, with not enough available. These are a step up from what a first-time buyer goes for, those who've bought a new build in a housing estate. We knew to aim a little bit higher, slightly higher spec to get slightly more, but nothing too fancy, to target buyers like second-time-buying families who were looking to upscale a bit, to upsize. And, thankfully, because Mick's in the trades, he had access to these amazing-looking bricks." She shakes her head. "I had no idea until we'd got into this project just how important bricks are, and what a difference they make, but it's about the little details – very straightforward, very basic, but which can make a huge difference in the finished product. You guys at White Box advise that we do the basics and that's exactly what we've done, and will continue to do."

"One thing I want to emphasise", Lloyd notes, "is that this deal you did was, in fact, available on the market. A lot of people looking at doing developments assume that the only good deals are found off-market, but that's not always the case. This featured planning for one house, but instead of just taking that as the one and only option, you gave it some thought as to how the site's value could be maximised beyond someone else's vision. You bought on the market, you converted it, you built it out, and you made it profitable. What would you estimate your profit to be on this site?"

"Our target was £197,000, although with materials going up in price over the last 12 months, it's actually probably been one of the most difficult periods that I can remember to build a house." Mick laughs, ruefully. "I picked that really well, what with COVID and such!

"But despite prices going through the roof", he adds, "we should still end up with something like £160,000 profit. It's possible it might be more than that, as haven't done the final calculations yet, not having all the bills in, but it's not going to hit our original target of… I think it was 32%?"

Lloyd taps the calculator on his desk. "The initial target was a 30–33% profit – again, from an on-the-market deal. So, unfortunately, you're only going to make a 27% profit!" Lloyd chuckles. "Seriously, that's an impressive amount."

"Actually", Annabel interjects, "Mick also hasn't yet factored in the fact that we haven't had to do any development finance on the drawdown, as that's all been raised by private finance, so we will have made a saving there. We bought it for cash and haven't done any drawdown at all. That will definitely factor into the profit calculation."

"I did work out the finance costs, and I think I'd estimated it would be something like £45,000 to £47,000 for all of it, the drawdown fees, the revaluation fees, all of it, and as Annabel notes, we haven't had to do any of that. So, yes, that will boost the profit."

"Regardless", says Andi, "it's an amazing result, and a real credit to you. You mentioned that you had to weather the pandemic and all of its restrictions, the biggest hike in building material costs that you've ever known in the 30 years you've been supplying other people, and despite those anomalies, you still managed to come out just shy of the profit you projected. That's really reassuring for anyone else looking to do what you're doing."

"We also ran out of cement on two occasions, because it was being rationed due to COVID-19 last year. It was limited to 25 bags for merchants but, because I'm in the trade, I know people and could get it sorted out. So, we only ran out for a few days, which didn't make any difference to us, thankfully."

"Neither of you", says Andi, "is brand new to property, but you've never done a development from the ground up before. Yet you obviously know a lot of people from the trade; you've been around it, you've seen other people do it, you've supplied materials for other people to do it. And, Annabel, you've worked with a lot of other types of investment properties: HMOs, single buy-to-lets, private investors, etc., but you weren't sure how to do it yourself. That's where the White Box training came in, as it gave you the confidence to move forward. And now look – you're at the end of your first development. How's that feel?"

"It's the most exciting thing I've ever been involved with", Annabel admits. "Thank you so much for all the information that you imparted to us in the training and throughout, because we literally have followed your advice, word for word, right down to putting together our investor packs, and putting together CGIs [computer-generated images] and the brochures for that, structuring offers – it really has made a huge difference. So, whilst we did have various challenges along the way, particular concerning materials, as Mick said, the actual process, thanks to you guys at White Box, was a lot easier than it otherwise would have been."

Mick nods. "I totally agree. There are two things that really stand out to me. One, which we learnt from you guys, concerns wealth – sharing deals. You taught us to share our deals, not to try to do them on our own but, instead, do a JV, a joint venture, with somebody, to partner up, because we both bring different things to the equation and to the build. That has proved to be a fantastic bit of advice for us. Annabel is amazing at what she does, the finance side of it. She knows loads of people and she's great in marketing. We combined her skills with mine, the skills to build the house itself, and we're confident now that, together, we can do tons of stuff. We're looking for sites at the moment, making offers, and we have a great partnership going forward, thanks to you. That's given me a great deal of confidence to continue ploughing forward."

"It's one thing to learn something; it's quite another to apply it", Lloyd points out with a smile. "We taught you, but it's you who have done the work.

"Now", he continues, "we've talked about the profit you're due to make, but let's talk about some of the challenges you've had, which Annabel mentioned, because it's not always plain sailing. One thing we at White Box want to emphasise is the reality of development. It's not always going to be straightforward and easy. There is a lot of money to be made, to be sure. But what sort of challenges have you had on the way?"

"Before Mick goes into the challenges we faced on the build side", Annabel says, "we had huge challenges actually getting it over the line, because we weren't working with the right team. We'd been working with the wrong solicitor, someone who was just hard work and made the process take a lot longer than necessary. That, and not going with the right lender, proved downright painful. We learned that lesson!

"We have since made the necessary changes", she says, "to ensure we're working with the right team in future projects. This is definitely a people business, and to line up the right people is paramount. Anything else gives rise to unnecessary hassles. If you've got the right people on your side, they're focused on helping, not setting up hurdles in front of you, wouldn't you say, Mick?"

"Definitely. We started off with a lender who made a small contribution to the land purchase. We'd purchased it for cash, but the lender financed a small percentage of it afterwards. However, Annabel sourced more investors and brought more money into the deal, thankfully, because both the lender and the solicitor were a nightmare to deal with – a lack of communication, no movement on their end; they just sat there!"

"You need to have a lawyer who chases you", Annabel suggests, "rather than you having to chase them. This solicitor has needed chasing the whole time, so we swore never again, and now, thankfully, we've found a good lawyer. Truly, your power team is absolutely crucial; it is definitely, again, just a key thing we've learned. And then, obviously, there were challenges in the build itself."

Mick nods. "Overall, the challenges on the build itself were small things, like the personalities on-site, between the different contractors rubbing each other the wrong way. Some of the contractors were falling out with the other contractors and I had to mediate, to remind them, 'Come on, guys, we've got a job to do here. Drop it.'"

"Counselling as well as building", Lloyd adds, with a knowing smile.

Mick smiles back, ruefully. "Exactly. There's that element to it, that you don't think about when you start, not until it crops up, hits you in the face, and you think, 'If I lose these two sets of contractors, how am I going to get this done?' Because you've got to book way in advance with your contractors, and keep in touch fairly regularly before the job is due to start, just to make sure they've remembered you, that they've still got you booked in, and they haven't got COVID or broken their leg, or whatever. And you just got to keep tabs on that beforehand. And even when you've got them on-site, that's not the end of it. It's like a playground", he says, chuckling. "You've got kids, different gangs of kids who, if they fall out with each other, you've had it! You've got to keep everything moving forward, and, fortunately, I've managed to do that."

"That's all part of the management side though, isn't it?" Andi says. "Just like your bad experience with that solicitor, you're not stuck with them; they don't have to be the one you'll use forever. You might have to replace a couple of them. But you've got to start somewhere, and those kinds of challenges are ones you just have to deal with as they happen.

"Property is ultimately a people's game", Andi adds, "whether you're working with professionals, the trades, whether you're making offers and working with agents, and selling – whatever. It all boils down to the relationships you have with people, doesn't it?"

"The other thing", Annabel adds, "that we weren't expecting, which Mick picked up on, was he was getting absolutely nowhere with the lawyer whatsoever. He just ghosted Mick for about a month, until we figured out that he responds better to females. So now I'm the only one who talks to the lawyer. Mick stays well out of that. At the same time, I don't think it would go down well on the site if I were the one talking to the 'kids'," she says, with a laugh. "Mick definitely has that covered."

"You'd be a distraction", Mick says, with a grin. "Those twelve guys wouldn't get anything done if you turned up."

Laughter

"I had never previously given any thought to the potential importance of the dynamic in having a female and a male duo", Annabel says. "Definitely, some people respond better to men, while others respond better to women. That was an interesting discovery for me", she admits.

Lloyd shakes his head. "It shouldn't be the case, but it's true, isn't it?"

"That's yet another reason why this is such a great partnership – that balance. If I had partnered with another man and we were trying to get results from that solicitor, who knows how long it would have taken to move things forward, if at all!"

Andy grins. "Luckily for me, Lloyd is very in touch with his feminine side, so we enjoy the same dynamic."

Laughter

"Returning to the subject of having a solid team on-site", Mick says, "if you get a good team of people together and manage things well, where each member, each contractor, knows what their job is, what their part is and they cooperate and coordinate well, it makes a world of difference. For example,

I'm sitting here now, participating in this podcast with you, while there are 12 contractors on our site working flat out, and things are getting done, and done properly, without my supervision. I know they are. That's how much confidence my team has given me."

"It does make a world of difference", Andi agrees. "It's quite common on sites to have contractors blame each other when things aren't getting done, instead of pulling together and taking responsibility. Ultimately, when they work together efficiently and cooperatively, things get done faster, they're ready to move on to other jobs more quickly, and they make more money as a result. It helps everyone to work well together. So, if you can have morning site meetings, if you can create the right culture and get them all to talk and work together harmoniously, they'll help you solve any on-site problems, and that makes your job – and everyone's job – easier."

"I couldn't agree more", Mick says. "There have been countless occasions when a contractor has said to me, 'Have you thought about [this] that's coming up?', or whatever they think I need to sort out because they don't want it holding up another contractor and it reminds me, yeah, I need to deal with that issue, which is going to take X amount of time to happen, so I need to plan ahead for it. It's great to have that level of overall awareness and efficiency among our team.

"There's also a level of accountability", he adds. "Sometimes you'll get a nudge that, hey, maybe that guy's working on a day rate but he's arriving at 10 a.m. and leaving at 3 p.m. It's in their best interest, as Andi said, to work efficiently, honestly, and productively. If the project is a success, that can generate future work for them."

"That's a product of the culture you've created", Lloyd says. "It sounds like you've built a great culture on-site among your team members.

"So, let's take a step back now, back to where you were when you both first decided to get into development. What was the reasoning behind it? Why did you want to do developments specifically?" Lloyd asks.

"Well, I'd wanted to do developments ever since I'd left school", Matt says, "but I always felt I needed to save up enough money to do it. My other businesses, before this, have always felt like a steppingstone towards that goal.

"I wish I'd had the chance to do your PDS course, your Property Developers Secrets course, years earlier, because it was only by taking your course that I learned about how to joint venture with people, the various finance methods I had no awareness of before. None of these projects have a single penny of my own money, because I brought Annabel, who has the know-how and contacts in finance, in at a very early stage to work with me on this. Whenever there are any money requirements, she's there to handle it – she's been absolutely brilliant with that." He shakes his head. "I feel like I wasted a good few years by not knowing this information earlier."

Andi says, "So, it's interesting that although you did, in fact, have some money that you could have put into this project, that you could have done it on your own, instead you leveraged Annabel's skills and learned how to leverage other people's money in a way that is far less restrictive on you. The problem when people look at just using their own money is that they are now limited to looking at sites they can afford, instead of being free to look for the best deal with the best returns because you can source other people for money to facilitate it. It really opens up options for you that would otherwise be out of reach."

"The COVID pandemic was, perversely, quite lucky for me in terms of timing, because the government were just handing out financial relief to businesses. We were eligible to receive the free £10,000 per premises for the business rate relief, plus the CBILS [Coronavirus Business Interruption Loan Scheme] loans, and so I had that reservoir to buy the site, without putting any of my own money in upfront. That's when Annabel came in, provided me money so we could split that site 50:50, and I then used that money to buy another site next door outright, on my own. I've since repaid the CBILS loans, and the financing that Annabel provided will get paid off when we build and sell the houses.

"So, instead of just struggling to do something all on my own, I've done two sites, retaining all of the profit in one, and half of the profit in the other. That's what you teach: share the deals and do joint ventures, so that you can do so much more with less risk in terms of personal investment."

"I've always been a firm believer in having a piece of the pie", Annabel says, "rather than the whole pie. I don't need the whole pie, and that approach has served me well. I never, in a million years, thought that I would get involved with building houses from scratch! I always thought it sounded good, that it would be nice to do, but I hadn't a clue where to start.

"I met Mick and his wife on a training course, several years ago", she continues, "and we started by doing business together with rental properties, HMOs, in the Midlands, which quickly demonstrated that we worked well together. We built a friendship from there, and then we got talking, and Mick said, 'Hey, I'm going to take this new-build course. You should come with me', to which I said okay. So, I did, and that's what got me here today. I have building relationships to thank for that, and Mick to thank for getting me involved in new builds. New builds, going forward, will definitely always be among my strategies within the property world. Without a doubt, it's been the most exciting strategy for me, amid all my years of being involved with rental properties, refurbs, back-to-bricks refurbs, and all of that. This is far more exciting. And I have Mick to thank for that, so thank you, Mick!"

"It certainly is proof", Lloyd says, "that activity creates opportunity".

"Going forward", Mick adds, "we'll be looking for sites to do together. Most of the sites I'll do in the future will be JVs, joint ventures, with Annabel. The only reason I'm doing this one site on my own is to get sufficient profit to buy land to build a house for my wife and me. That's the only reason. And if we continue to do joint ventures, we can do a lot more projects together. Annabel's just so good in terms of securing investors using her network."

"Plenty of pieces of the pie for everyone to fill up on!" Lloyd says, nodding. "You don't need the whole pie to feel satisfied. So", he adds, "what advice would you give anyone contemplating getting into developments?"

Mick doesn't hesitate. "To do your course!"

Andi and Lloyd chuckle.

"Seriously though", Mick says, "my advice, in a nutshell, is: Do the White Box course, absolutely, without a shadow of a doubt, and do not delay! As I said earlier, I regret having lost some years previously by not having been well informed, for thinking that I couldn't start until I'd saved up enough hard-earned money from my business to do developing on my own. Absolute rubbish, that was! But you, at White Box, taught us not to do that, not to focus on using our own money and, instead, use OPM, other people's money. It's incredible how one change of perspective opens your eyes to all of the bigger opportunities that are out there, waiting for you, that you would never have otherwise considered."

"I think", Annabel adds, "that the more you talk to people – and it doesn't have to be solely within the property arena – the more you talk to people, particularly now, the more it becomes evident just how much money there is in the system. Actually, right now, there are a lot fewer quality options in which to invest one's money, in terms of the entire financial universe, not just property. As a result, there's a lot more money in search of investment vehicles than there are good investments. So, when you find a good investment, the money will flow; when you find a good deal, the money is just there. Once you start to work with private lenders, once they see that the model works, and you've built that relationship, the money will just continue to flow towards you. Some of our investors have already told us that we can keep reinvesting their money, some have said for another two years, some have said for five years, and some have said to keep it indefinitely, to just keep reinvesting it in our projects. We've got one person lined up who has the cash sitting there, ready for the next site, a site which we're now in the process of securing. And because, again, our focus has been on building relationships, we've built one with a vendor from whom we've already bought two plots. They can see from the investor packs and the offer packs that we've put together, the packs that we learned to put together in the White Box PDS course, that we know what we're talking about. So, now, this vendor has said he only wants to sell his last plot to us, and he wants to set it up as an option agreement where we guarantee to make the purchase upon receiving the planning permission.

"Again, it all comes back to building those relationships. It really is a very exciting time to be in developments", Annabel says. "Thank you for everything you've taught us, including the monthly networking gatherings. I'll be at the next one."

"Yes, thanks for the superb education!" Mick echoes.

"Well, your success really has been impressive", Lloyd says, "and it certainly sounds as if there's plenty more that lies ahead. Thank you for sharing your journey with us and our listeners."

JAMES ADAMS – FAIRHOLM ESTATES

https://m.facebook.com/FairholmEstates/

Instagram - @fairholmestatesuk

https://www.linkedin.com/company/fairholm-estates/

James Adams is a landlord, investor, and developer based in Bristol. Initially, he focused on HMO conversions, but is now transitioning more towards development. James has always been a very calculated person, something we noticed when we first met him on the PDS course. James is a sensible character who doesn't mind giving something a go and getting stuck in. It took a while for him to get his momentum going, but once he found his team, the opportunities came soon after.

James is currently building out his first site and is set to make a decent profit from it. It will certainly earn him more money than his traditional HMO investment strategy would, and possibly, a lot more easily too. James is also the host of The Developers Network in Bristol, so if you're reading this and would like to check it out, flip to the back of this book for current locations and information on how to participate.

As they take their seats, Lloyd says, "Welcome to the White Box podcast. Would you introduce yourself to the audience, and share with them how you first got started and where you are right now, what you're doing in the development world right now?"

"Well, up until about a year ago, I focused exclusively on HMO conversions, mainly structural refurbishments for the student market, up in Manchester. Over the past 12 months,

I've been shifting more towards development, particularly one new-build development, closer to home, in Bristol, whilst still keeping up the HMO work in Manchester. So, I've been educating myself during the last 12 months, sourcing a lot of sites to find something the right size and suited to what I want to do."

James leans forward in his chair. "I found a site about 10 weeks ago, made an offer, and it was accepted about seven or eight weeks ago. So, right now, I'm doing all of the site due diligence for that, tendering and everything else that goes along with the site. I've also got quite a few HMO projects on the go as well, up in Manchester."

"I remember when you took the White Box Property Developers Secrets course", Andi says, "just over a year ago. At the end you went off to consider your options with developments and decide whether it was the right step for you to take. You rang me up, told me you were doing an HMO conversion, and asked if, even if you weren't involved with the Mastermind program at the time, could we have a little chat, as you wanted to get some advice. That was probably the start your journey into development."

James nods. "I remember. It was a very stressful period, right before Christmas. If there's one thing I've learned over the last year, which you had emphasised, it's that a lot of what's involved in development has to do with mindset. At the time it seemed like a very difficult situation, with lots of issues to solve, and I really appreciated your input, Andi. It was very helpful then, because I was – and still am – working on my own. I don't really have anybody as a soundboard for things like that, whereas you have a lot of experience in construction, with much bigger problems to solve. So, it was really useful to have your guidance at the time." He chuckles. "Looking back now, with all I've learned so far, it was arguably a rather easy problem to solve. My mindset really has advanced in the last 12 months, since taking your PDS course."

Andi nods. "I agree. Your journey over this past year has been nothing short of amazing. Like you say, it's typically just a case of talking it through, of realising that the challenges you're facing aren't insurmountable at the end of the day. By being part of the Mastermind program over the last 12 months, you've enjoyed having that sounding board you needed, that guidance, not just from a lawyer but from others on their Mastermind journey and mentors. And so, with that, you're better able to solve the kinds of issues that arise, and do it a lot more quickly."

Lloyd says, "This book is all about is illustrating the property journeys that people are taking after feeling more confident once they've taken the PDS course. You were already in property. You mention mindset, which, as we at White Box say, is key, because many property courses discuss the technical aspects of developments, but they don't talk about the mindset change that developers need. Because it is challenging, it will be tough. That's why we, at White Box, dissect that and explain that it's not as easy as some would like to pretend it is. You're more likely to be successful if you're prepared for the challenges, when you know that others have faced those same challenges and have come out profitably on the other side.

"What's great about you, James, is that you really take in all of the information we provide and proceed through it, step by step", Lloyd adds. "Obviously, you were in property before this, doing HMO conversions, so you get that part. But when we talk about situations, when we say, 'James, this is what you need to do now', you go and do it. That's the thing – you do it. Step by step, you do it. It's the strength of that new mindset. Others might hesitate. But you stay focused, and every single week you check in and say, 'This is what I've done', and share the results for everyone's benefit.

"So, tell us about this new site you've got", he prompts, "the one your offer was just accepted on a month or two ago. Because that's what this book about, not just outcomes but following people like yourself who have projects underway, at various stages. By the way, if anyone wants to follow your journey, James, these are the social media tags to source. But if you would, explain the deal you're about to get underway on."

"Sure. So, recently I've done a lot of on- and off-market site searches, mostly focused on identifying a large volume of sites, but I found that the prices didn't necessarily stack up. Despite that, I'm still making quite a few offers, without paying much attention to the list prices. But it was after a sourcing day, over in your guy Matt's office, who loves doing deals and is very good at finding them, when we went through the different tactics to use, one in particular jumped out at me: using the planning portal. It proved enormously useful for a number of reasons – it shows which professionals are putting forward planning applications, what developers are active in the area, what projects are getting the knock-back, what types of projects are getting approved. So, I found the portal really handy in a number of ways.

"Basically, I went back through planning applications over the preceding four or five months, and trained my VA, my virtual assistant, to help me do that." He laughs, admitting, "I didn't know what a VA was before White Box, to be honest. And she's been great. I speak to her every day, as she's a valuable member of my team. So, on the portal we found this particular site which already had an application for full planning that was pending. It's a classic development site, a bungalow, a low-density site with a planning application for four three-bed houses, that just jumped off the map at me as an ideal one to do. I wrote a letter to the vendor, but didn't hear anything back for some time. Then, out of the blue he messaged me. He'd had another deal that had fallen through because the council was taking ages to make a decision and so the other developer moved on. We spoke and I sent through an offer pack to him fairly quickly, given how well it stacked up compared to a lot of deals that just don't stack up." He grins. "I was quite keen to get in there. He rejected my first offer, which he said was less than what the previous developer had offered. We went back and forth, before eventually agreeing to a price. I got an exclusivity agreement to permit me to work through all the site due diligence, which was extended as of a couple of days ago, because there's still more to do."

James shakes his head with a smile. "One thing I've learned is that everything takes longer than you think it's going to. Everyone, whether it's a surveyor or people doing ground investigations, lawyers, they all have their lead times. Definitely a lesson I've learned! So, even though we haven't exchanged on it yet, I've learned a massive amount about it, just up to this point, in terms of everything that needs to be done."

Lloyd nods. "That's an important point. We always remind people that things don't happen instantly in development – you're not going to become a millionaire overnight. And as this is a commercial purchase, it takes a bit longer, with more due diligence required before you can purchase the site. In the long run, though, while development may take a bit longer than other wealth-building strategies out there, it's arguably more rewarding. It's not a question of getting out what you put into it; instead, our experience is that you get back more than what you put in. But it does take time.

"Can you share with us what are the figures on this deal? What are you looking at GDV-wise, the gross development value, and profit-wise?" Lloyd asks.

James thinks a moment. "The GDV is probably somewhere about £1.55–1.6 million." He chuckles. "Agents are telling me it'll be more, but I prefer to use my judgement. I'm hoping to clear £300,000 profit. But there are, as with all developments, still some unknowns, GDV being one. Another is the ground – we're a bit uncertain as to the substructure we're going to use, because of the area that the site's in. And we're not 100% sure what the drainage solution will be. So, all that influences costs. Ballpark, though, we're hoping to make £300,000 profit. Certainly, as you point out, it takes time, and with a new build in particular, it's a later payoff. It takes a lot of groundwork in advance to hopefully achieve that payoff."

"Given that you've been as engaged with White Box at the level you have, and how frequently you participated in my group", Andi says, "I've been witness to your journey from the start, the fears and obstacles you've shared along the way. I could see that once you dealt with other issues that temporarily claimed your attention and could realign your focus to prioritise this in your life, you effectively applied your time with White Box as a form of accountability as well as education, to help keep you focused and on track."

James nods as Andi continues.

"In early 2021, I set you some monthly tasks to achieve. Maybe it's your background", he says, chuckling, "having been a teacher, but you responded positively to that, and in every month since, you've tried to hit those targets we set in our sessions. You chart what you spend your time on, some months on the HMO side of things and others more on development, depending on what you're focusing on each month, and each and every week you send me that accounting. How would you describe the journey you've been on?"

James thinks a moment. "Well, as you pointed out, when I joined the Mastermind sessions, there were other things that needed my attention outside of property, but I was facing a learning curve as well. Being that I was new to development, and knew so little about it, I had to find my footing and spend time learning what it was that I needed to do. For me, because I was also working for myself, and it was just me, I had to calculate how best to allocate my time in order to use it most efficiently. I was also home-schooling, which was taking up quite a bit of time." He smiles. "But then it dawned on me that I could just get up earlier in the day!

I realised I could carve out time early in the morning when it's nice and quiet and I don't have to do other things, which enabled me to be more productive. Starting work earlier became a good habit, one that was definitely influenced by people in the Mastermind sessions, because there are some extremely hard-working people there who do put in a lot of hours. You're not going to get big payoffs in development, or anything else, unless you're determined to put in the hours.

"So, yeah, the time accountability charting proved good

for me because now I can see how I'm balancing my time between my responsibilities as an HMO landlord and what I need to accomplish in the development side of things. I could see, in black and white, that I needed more of my hours and activity to be spent on development; otherwise, it wasn't going to happen. So, that became my aim for the year, to find a development site. It was very simple – that's what I wanted to do. So, while I'm ultimately accountable to myself, what with being on my own, having external checks unquestionably helped me stay focused and on track. As you pointed out", he says with a laugh, "coming from a teaching background, I'm used to a timetable.

"I do agree", he adds, "that what you get out of anything is reflected by what you put in. I'm not saying you have to double the hours you spend working, and work through the night or whatever. I discovered I could do it well once I started using my time more efficiently, and by focusing on the right things. Working smarter, not harder, as they say. I've made sure that as well as doing my development stuff, I've made time for my family, because they're one of the main reasons as to why I'm in property, and why I want to be a master of my time. I also make time for fitness and good health, because it naturally makes me sharper and more productive, both in site finding and overall."

"I agree", Andi says. "I've seen you transform your mindset, your morning routine, the fitness and wellness improvement over the last 12 months. Was that something you foresaw happening in being part of the Mastermind program, something that White Box, or us personally, influenced you in? Or did it just manifest naturally as part of the journey, do you think?"

"When I joined the Mastermind, to be honest, I hadn't envisioned nearly any of the many overall benefits I've reaped from it", James admits. "Yes, I'd anticipated benefiting from all of the knowledge base: planning, project management, site finding, finance, and all of that stuff. But what I hadn't contemplated were what are arguably even bigger rewards – being inspired by other participants, by the mentors, and changing the way I think, raising my aspiration level. I hadn't considered what a huge plus it would be to be part of a like-minded network. Networking isn't really a thing in the same way in teaching as it is in development, where it's paramount. It's just been a huge bonus in developing the right mindset and feeling as inspired as I do now. You can't put a price on that."

Lloyd nods. "I think a lot of people underestimate the power of the community in the Mastermind program. A lot of people are quick to rule out its importance, thinking, Oh, it's not for me, or It's too expensive, or It's not the right time – we hear these all the time. But, instead, you've embraced it, immersed yourself in it. Listening to you now, only 12 months since you started and first told us that you were interested in development but didn't know anything about it, you're now talking knowledgeably about things like tackling drainage on your new site, how you need to sort out your planning conditions and such – this is you, just 12 months later! We find that a lot of people don't always look back on the journey they've taken, what they've been through, what they've accomplished; instead, they're relentlessly focused on what lies ahead: trying to be better, to do more, to get to the next level. But reflection on how far you've come is a good thing to do periodically. With that in mind, let's look back to when you first started, when you first thought about get into development. What were your biggest fears about doing a development?"

"My initial fears were quite basic", James admits. "Like the ground itself." He laughs. "Doing refurbishments is a different ballgame to breaking ground on a new build – buying the land and all the things that come at that basic level. One fear was what if I bought a plot of land and only found out afterwards that there existed obstacles that would prevent me from moving forward and now I've made this investment that isn't going to pay off." He laughs again. "I was even worried about archaeology! And the building element itself, that was also a concern. Fear of the unknown, really, is what it boiled down to. I wasn't sure what I was really capable of. I'd thought, maybe, that I might start with converting a commercial building vs. undertaking a new build. It seemed like a natural step forward from HMOs. It took about four to six months for me to acknowledge that I'd already done a fair bit of conversion and that what I wanted was the experience new build.

"Once I had the knowledge I gained from White Box, it actually was not that daunting. I just needed more knowledge about how the process works, which I got with White Box. It was more myths, or fear of the unknown, that made me hesitate."

Lloyd nods. "Yes, it's a common misconception that people think commercial conversions are easier than new builds. Both have their ups and the downs, but with the inception of a new build, it's so much easier than being limited by existing walls and features. Commercial conversions tend to be easier to find, in our experience, but can often prove more challenging to convert than starting fresh. So, it took you about four to six months to assure yourself that a new build might not be as hard as you feared initially."

"That side of it, the thought of actually digging a hole, building pits and foundations and houses a year ago was not something I'd imagined I was even capable of."

"James, should we talk about the funding side of things?" Andi asks. "For example, when you first started out, how did you feel about raising such a big chunk of money from other private investors? How did you feel about it, initially, and how do you feel about now – how has your mindset shifted in terms of that?"

"Well, I'd always leaned towards private financing before I started. My journey has probably been slower than some because I'd always relied on refinancing vs. finding private investors. But one of the many useful things White Box has taught me is that private investors can be such a useful thing to have in the background, there to help support your business.

"Initially, I was reluctant to approach family and friends, as I was hesitant to even tell people about what I was doing, thinking that I wasn't doing this professionally, or that I might not be up to the job, the self doubt that we all tend to have. But in the last year, having gained experience and become more confident with what I've learned through White Box, with this new project I've been more confident about approaching friends and family to invest in this deal. Because White Box has taught me about things like how to put together a solid investor pack that provides all of a deal's ins and outs, that has enhanced my credibility to where I'm comfortable presenting myself as a professional. If my potential investors go through the pack, they can see a well-thought-out, well-planned project vs. some hare-brained scheme. When people invest with you, they're putting their trust in you. By preparing carefully, as I have now learned to do, I am legitimately earning that trust.

On the development finance side, what can put you off are the rates and fees, because it's completely different to vanilla buy-to-let or HMO lending. Rates on development finance are much higher. Having the finance brokerage Pilot Fish in the background as mentors been massively useful, because development finance is quite complicated relative to a straightforward mortgage. But, again, once you get your head around it, once you've become familiar with its ins and outs, it's no longer the scary proposition it once was. You just need to feed it into your modelling to make sure the deal stacks up; it needs to be reflected in your appraisal. I've learned so much from White Box about the finance side of this."

"It's all about adding to the tools in your toolbox, isn't it?" Andi suggests. "Not every finance package suits every deal. It's about knowing enough to calculate what financial structure fits best for a given deal, and as you noted, Pilot Fish, which provide development finance, guide our network very well. White Box also has people like Scott Marshall, the Managing Director of development lender Roma Finance, who built the business up, who have been very good friends and mentors to the White Box community. We get to see how it works from their perspective, and learn more about which tools fit, and which lenders fit, because no one lender fits every deal. When you come more confident with the finance end of things and skilled at assembling an investor package to present your investment proposition, it's easier for others as well as yourself to see how it all fits together."

"That's exactly it", Lloyd says, nodding.

"Scott's been a big help", James agrees. "He actually lives in my village, where I grew up, so we're from the same part of the world. Scott's very knowledgeable, and how he's built up his business is inspiring as well."

"So", says Lloyd, "it really has been a bit of an amazing journey, so far, and this is still just the beginning for you in the development world. And now ahead of you is that £300,000 potential profit, which is likely even more of a realistic number now, as GDVs have risen slightly since you started. Things might change as we get further into 2022, but right now a £300,000 projection is realistic. But tell us now: Where do you see yourself going with all of this? What inspired you to do developments in the first place?"

"I'll likely take the profit and reinvest it in my next deal, as my thoughts are already shifting towards my pipeline and what we'll do next." He grins. "I might treat myself to something, if I'm lucky enough to make some profit, but reinvesting it, and continuing to build momentum, get the pipeline going, get some more deals going, that's where my focus will be.

"In terms of why I got into development in the first place, I think it was twofold. One is that in my other business, doing HMO conversions, the margins have become more and more difficult to extract. That's partly due to the fact that they've proved to be expensive refurbishment projects. It's difficult to buy cheaply in the right areas, and HMOs have become a very competitive market, with lots of players. The time needed for those versus developments, the risk/reward ratio, made me think I should diversify, that given the headaches inherent in a big HMO conversion, my time could be better spent on a new build, where although there's more involved in it, the payoffs are significantly higher.

"That's the first reason", he says. "The second reason is that, for me, developments seemed the pinnacle of property – it's about building, making homes from scratch for people, how that would make me feel once I'd completed a project. To make somewhere nice for somebody to live is a major dream for me to aspire to.

"So, the first reason is business related, while the second is my vision. I'm passionate about property and again, for me, development is the pinnacle. I wanted to see if I could challenge myself to do it. And that passion is why I willingly invested both time and money to educate myself and join a solid, valuable network to see me through future projects. White Box hasn't disappointed."

"Well, James, you really embraced everything we have to offer at White Box", Andi says. "You've taken it all on board, grasped that being a developer is for life – it's not just to do one deal, make a £300,000 profit, and see yourself on the beach on some tropical island somewhere after just one deal, somehow able to retire and never have to work again. It's not a means to an end. It is the end goal, to keep that pipeline fuelled and flowing, to sustain that momentum as you so eloquently put it.

"We're passionate about property", Andi says, "and we want it to continue to be our journey, to continue learning and doing and growing for the rest of our lives. That's what being a real developer is. The way you explained your second point makes me even prouder to be a developer, that I'm providing homes to my and other communities. As Lloyd said, it's important to occasionally pause and look back at what we've done, the contributions we've made, the developments we've achieved. These are things we all deserve to be proud of. And it's great to see you on the start of your life's journey with it, too."

Lloyd nods. "What's great, too, about building houses is that they'll still be standing long after we're gone. There's a reassuring permanence to them, that when the person who's occupying them moves on, someone else is excited to come in to enjoy what you've created. So, it's a philosophy in a way, as well as engaging in a supportive network."

"Yes, I like the idea of it being a legacy", James says.

"Before we wrap up, is there any advice, James, that you have for anyone who's still on the fence in thinking about development?"

"I would say, 'Don't underestimate what's required. You need to be somebody who's got a passion for property. It needs to be something that's always in your head, that you think about a lot, that you're really interested in, knowing and loving that it has lots of moving parts. By that I mean, if you're somebody who is interested in all the different aspects that pertain to property, then it's definitely a good thing to consider. But while it's important not to underestimate what's involved, it's just as important not to permit yourself to become paralysed with fear about the unknowns. That's where White Box can help. As we said before, there are quite a few myths surrounding property development, but once you invest time and effort into educating yourself on the ins and outs of it, that knowledge builds confidence, and it becomes much less intimidating, because it's no longer fear of the unknown. Instead, you've taken the time and made the effort to define what it is, what's involved, and you're going in with your eyes open. There's a lot to take in, lots of different things to learn, but it's incredibly rewarding, a truly great career for someone with passion."

Lloyd grins. "And if you could sum up White Box in a few sentences, what would you say?"

James doesn't hesitate. "I'd say that it's a stellar community, one that truly adds value for the people within its active network, within the White Box family. It's done an incredible amount for me, far beyond what I'd ever imagined, and I can't really express my gratitude fully to all of the people on the Mastermind and the mentors who have helped me so much this past year. Incalculable."

"Well, it's certainly been a pleasure helping you so far", Lloyd says, "and we're looking forward to helping you in this next deal, and all of the deals after that! Thanks very much, James."

FAHD KHAN & SREELAL HARILAL – PROVIDENT HOMES

http://linktr.ee/providenthomes

This is an interesting chapter because not only did Fahd Kahn and Sreelal Harilal meet on the Property Developers Secrets course and start their business together from that but they teamed up with us to develop their first project of 24 flats. As a beginner to property, taking on 24 flats for your first project wouldn't be easy, unless you have a team with experience. We have provided them with this experience to get started and they have since gone on to do some amazing projects. After all, it's not about how you start; it's about starting – that's more important.

"Hello, and welcome, Fahd and Sreelal, from Provident Homes", Lloyd says. "Let's talk about your story, how you got going, how you got started. What are you actually doing at the moment? What are your headline figures for the deals you're doing?"

"We've got a pipeline of projects", Fahd says, "some of which are currently in development, and some about to start. A project total of £7 million in GDV – gross development value – that's active developments. We've got other projects –we're working with housing associations – and projects we flipped for planning uplift, so, in terms of total property transactions that we've been involved in, probably in excess of £10 million.

"When we're talking developments, talking in terms of millions of pounds is normal. But when you're just starting out, that sounds a bit scary, doesn't it, thinking in terms of millions of pounds?"

"That's true", says Sreelal, chuckling. "For me, just a few years back, it was hard to conceive of that, but now my friends are amazed by how casually I think in terms of millions."

"And, of course, we talk millions, but profit-wise it's not millions", Lloyd notes. "It's tens of thousands, typically, but, yes, in terms of actual value of property, it is millions.

"Now, we're working on a deal together", Lloyd adds, "into which we'll go into detail in a moment, which is, itself, £3.8 million. But tell us first how you got into property, because you've been in it for a while now."

"I'm a dentist", Fahd says, "but my dad was a small-time developer in London – Croydon – and so back when I was just a kid, my toys were tools. My dad always took me to sites, to refurbs and conversions, and every house we ever bought and lived in, we'd always refurbish it, sell it, and move on to the next home. So you could say that property is kind of in our blood, in our DNA.

"By the time I got into my teens", Fahd adds, "I was learning more trades and project-managing other people, and was involved in some family projects. The jewel in the crown at the time was probably a detached property that we owned that, in a former life, was a nursing home, then a 10-bed, a bed sit/HMO, and then we got planning permission to add another storey on top, which added six apartments.

"That said, I saw a lot of risk in working with my dad, so I got my dentistry degree in 2010 and focused on my dentistry career for the next few years, but nonetheless I had a burning desire to get back into property, but with the added benefit of education – I knew I wanted to do it on a far more professional level.

"I started off with homes-under-the-hammer-type properties", Fahd says, "and made some mistakes in auctions. The numbers I'm dealing with today are a distant leap from the figures we were dealing with back then, like a ground-rent investment for £15,000, some land in Milton Keynes for £50,000, and they were garbage, to be honest. We're dealing with a whole different scale in property now, all made possible through networking and education."

"That's key, though, isn't it?" Lloyd says. "The size of the deal isn't what matters. If it's an uneducated deal, meaning you don't really understand what it is you're doing, it's likely going to be garbage. If it's an educated deal, a deal you understand, size doesn't really matter in terms of outcome. The value, when we talk about millions, is nothing more than just an extra zero tacked onto the end.

"When you talk to your friends and you're talking in terms of millions, you have to remember that it is just a zero. That's what helped Andi and me, when we first started. A guy told us, 'The deals you're looking at, don't be scared by them, because it's just a zero'. We thought about it and said, 'Okay, yeah, I get that'.

"So", Lloyd continues, "getting back to your story, Fahd – you first met me on a webinar, wasn't it?"

"Yes, and that really opened my eyes to what property education had to offer. I started to realise how much I didn't actually know about property. I understood bricks and mortar, I understood trades, but all of the different strategies and how you can monetize property, none of that I knew.

"So, at that time", Fahd explains, "I did a couple of courses and I had just joined the YPN, and on a webinar this guy called Lloyd Girardi was talking about these developments he'd done – he'd built these 11 houses in Irthlingborough. I was, like, no way! I had just moved from London to Northamptonshire, and we'd bought our first house in Irthlingborough. My friends call it Middle Earth", Fahd jokes, "because no one's ever heard of it. And this chap has just built 11 houses in Irthlingborough? Here I'd thought nobody had ever even heard of the place! So that convinced me: If someone's doing developments here, then I've got to meet them, I've got to find out how they've done what they've done, and how they got to where they have. So, I started following White Box quite closely."

"Very closely!" Lloyd says.

Laughter.

"Let's explain that one", Lloyd says, laughing. "We talk about following, and a lot of people follow me on social media – on Twitter, on Instagram, etc., but you followed us literally. So, this guy used to turn up at my kid's nursery. I mean, he's got a kid as well", Lloyd hastily adds, amid laughter. "But you were there, and we kept seeing each other, and then one day you said, 'I think you go to the same nursery, and I've just watched your webinar. I think you're Lloyd'. And I said, 'Yeah, it's me.' And it just progressed from there, didn't it?"

"That's right", Fahd says. "For anyone who subscribes to the Law of Attraction, when you set your mind to something, you start to see that something manifest in all sorts of places. So, I did the Discovery Day with White Box, straight after I'd done the webinar, as you'd advertised that Discovery Day, so I booked that straightaway, wanting to find out what you guys were all about. That's where I met Sreelal. In the subsequent months, I bumped into you at various different places, and then I enrolled my son into Wellingborough School. Lo and behold, I bumped into Andi there, as all three of his kids go to Wellingborough School. So, he thought, Okay, so you've moved on from stalking Lloyd to stalking me now. And then I wanted to find a gym, began researching all the different gyms, and decided I'd try this one particular gym out, and at my first session at the gym, who do I see? Andi! And so now I've become known as The White Box Stalker."

"We say copy what we do, follow what we do, but not literally!" Lloyd says, grinning.

More laughter.

"But no, we don't mind", Lloyd assures Fahd. "You've done well out of it! So, tell us your story, Sreelal. How did you get started? Obviously, we first met at the networking event that we used to run."

"Exactly", Sreelal says. "I met you guys in Northampton. I used to be a regular at your events, thinking, This really looks nice, what these guys are doing. But for me it was hard to believe that something's right, that property would be right for me to do. When you don't know what you don't know, is hard to conceive of taking such a thing on. I was thinking, No, this is just probably the course making it seem possible, but I can't do it. I'm just a software engineer. How am I supposed to do development?

"It took me a few months to get into it, to start believing I could do that. Then I experienced a mindset change. I did some White Box training. I had always wanted to get into property, but I'd been very passive about it. I did some HMOs in Hamilton Keynes, but I couldn't motivate myself to deal with the figures and all, because I was doing okay with my job. But I started thinking more and more about development. If I could get this working, I thought, it would be a massive achievement, and a way to give back, as well – it's going to be really impactful. That's when I did the White Box training, I came for the land sourcing that you did, met Fahd, and we kept in touch. And we started Provident Homes. But it all started thanks to you guys. We came to the PDS, the Property Developers Secrets, and did the Mastermind networking, which is a constant, every-month session. When you're working especially, it's not easy, but it keeps returning you to the mindset you need, to stay focused on what you want to be doing. The accountability is in place with that. It took the better part of a year to find the right deal, and it was frustrating at times."

"Yeah, you went through quite a few", Lloyd recalls, "and that's what we teach is the norm, of having to go through a few deals. You've got to kiss a few frogs to get the right one and—"

"Well, we certainly kissed a few frogs!" Fahd interjects.

Laughter

"It's part of the education", Lloyd admits. "But, going back to the network meeting you mentioned, I remember you being there. There was one time when you had about 20 questions—"

"I always have questions", Sraleel says, laughing.

"Which is fine", Lloyd reassures him. "We were happy to answer them. If you're not sure about something, the best way we can help you is to try to answer your questions. It's not us to just fob you off and say, 'Just do it'. We wanted to help you, and so we set up that land sourcing day for you – which is the only one we've ever done to this day – it was a bit of a test to see how we could help people. And that's essentially where you both met. You didn't really know each other before that, but found you had a bit in common. And Provident Homes came out of that.

"Now", Lloyd says, "let's talk about the frogs you've kissed, because there are always challenges in development, as everyone who's doing it knows".

"It took us a while, as Sreelal said, to find our first deal", Fahd says. "The deal that we eventually signed up for was at an auction, to buy some land in Corby. The proposal there seemed quite black and white. It's a small parcel of land, part of a larger development for 5,000 homes. Outline planning had already been granted, Phase One had essentially been completed – this was the only parcel in Phase One that hadn't yet been implemented. So, it was just a Reserved Matters application.

"We looked at it, and the person who was fronting that deal was a developer and an architect, very, very experienced. When we looked at the numbers, things were tight, but we thought that, with this guy's experience, it was doable and would also almost be like an additional mentorship by someone who is far more experienced than us and we'd learn from it. So, we signed up for the deal. It took us 18 months, because we initially had planning refused, which was a challenge. Eventually, we got planning for 18 houses, but by the time we reached the point of starting, or thinking about developing, we realized that this particular joint venture was not all it was cracked up to be.

"We did some more research and we found things in this person's background that we hadn't been made aware of, and alarm bells started to ring. It was a very, very difficult decision that we had to come to, to sell our very first project, and it was at the start of COVID-19. So, one, COVID was an added risk because we didn't what was going to happen, and, two, we thought there was a major risk in continuing any further, and taking massive lending with PGs involved, with a potential partner who could become insolvent, whom we didn't fully trust.

"That was a very, very difficult 18 months that we went through" he adds, "as we started to learn that person's true colours, and it made us very wary of entering into another JV."

"It's sensible, though, to analyse a deal like that, and it was your first, so you could have just as easily said let's just do it, let's take the risk, let's take a chance, just to get some experience. But you saw some red flags and chose not to move forward, ultimately. But that experience has helped, because it's led you to what you're doing now, and taught you something about doing joint ventures. Now, I don't know about these joint venture partners you've got now...", Lloyd jokes, referring to the deal they're currently doing together.

Laughter

"But it's taught you to analyse each deal a little bit more, hasn't it?" Lloyd prompts. "Let's talk about the deal you're doing now."

"Well", says Fahd, "that same year we went to Bali on a White Box retreat. Lloyd had asked me to come the year before, but I didn't see the value of going – it was a long way to go and didn't strike me as anything but an expensive holiday. But he kept insisting it wasn't a holiday, and that it was hard to quantify what the benefits would be, but that it would be valuable.

"I'm quite a sceptic", Fahd adds, "coming from a medical profession, where everything's evidence based. I don't just take people at their word. For me, actions speak louder than words, so I assess people based on what they've achieved and how they live. I'd been to courses run by others before, and there's always been an upsell, there's always a catch. Having experienced that, I closely monitored what the guys at White Box were about. And because we live in the same town – seeing them at the gym, seeing them at our kids' school – I realized that what you see is what you get with them – that they're the same in the course, during the Mastermind, as they are in day-to-day life, always operating with an open-door mindset. They've always got time for people, and they generally want to help. It took a while for me to lose my scepticism and start to see the value of working with them.

"So, I agreed to go to the to the retreat the following year", Fahd says, "and we discussed the challenges we'd had on our first site. Then we looked at the potential sites we'd identified. We'd identified this one site on Mill Road, a derelict factory in Wellingborough, five minutes from my house on the route I drive each day to drop my kids at school. I would see it and imagine that, one day, maybe when I'm 50 or 60 and I've retired, how I would love to take on a project like that. I've got a massive interest in architecture and in history, and this did really ignite my passion. But I never, ever thought it could be done without bags of cash and loads of experience.

"Still, I mentioned the site when we were in Bali, as it was available, we'd looked at it and had spoken to a couple of contractors, but there were just too many unknowns and it made us feel way out of our depth. But in getting to know Andi and Lloyd and their getting to know us, by the end of that retreat, we decided to have a look at it together. Fast forward, and we're now in the best JV we've ever been in!"

"It's a deal that we've learned from as well", Lloyd says. "It's a big deal for us, and not the most straightforward."

"Not for the faint-hearted", Fahd concurs.

"But this is your first real development project, isn't it?" Lloyd notes. "And one of the challenges you had, one that anyone would have had, not just you, is that you hadn't a track record of doing many conversions, and a track record is something you need in order to secure funding. You did have a contractor looking at it already. So, yeah, we looked at it together and said, we'd be happy to joint venture, that it was an opportunity that we could help you with that would help us as well, because we had some spare time in the build side. So, we came on as a contractor and a joint venture partner, which gave you the necessary track record to get the funding.

"Tell us, from your point of view, how's the site going?" he asks. "It's nearly finished – we're getting there, I know, and it's been a learning curve for us, certainly."

"It's been a learning curve", Sreelal agrees. "But I think that without you guys, it would have been a very big challenge for us. The biggest risks are getting the right contractor and having the necessary track record to get the funding, as you said, but by joint venturing with you, the project has been really done to high standards, as evidenced by our show homes. We already have exits almost started on this now."

"Yes, at the time we're recording this", Lloyd says, "we've got offers on the table. We're just trying to push them up a little bit to where we need or want them to be. It is exciting."

"Really exciting", Sreelal says. "And having done this deal, people are taking us much more seriously. I see it even when calling agents, once we say we're calling about the building in Wellingborough, Mill Road, that 9 Mill Road is our project."

"And it's not made the profit that we'd set out when we first started", Lloyd notes. "The COVID pandemic has been an issue, we've had build costs increase, as we had to put so much steel in that building – which is ironic, given that it was a steel factory at one point!"

Laughter

"We've had to put more steel in", Lloyd says, "but it's been a steppingstone to other projects, hasn't it? You've got some more sites on the go from that as well, haven't you? One key point I want to note here though is that with all of this going on, you guys are still employed full-time, outside of this."

"Four days a week, yes. For this, it's Fridays and weekends and mostly nights."

"That's key to doing deals", Lloyd says. "If you haven't got a lot of time to do them, then find someone who does have the time. We always say that, as a developer, you are the conductor of the orchestra, not a musician. We came in as the contractors – we're the builders, so we take care of the project work while you guys are out there finding more deals. It's been a successful joint venture, I would say. You've been a part of it without having to spend too much time on it."

Sreelal nods. "That's one of the things you guys teach as well, that it's not critical to know everything when you get into property; it's about who you know, building the right team by networking, and identifying who's the best at something. I still remember when I first began going to the Northampton meeting, I was too intimidated to talk to the people there, because I hadn't done any deals and these were developers and such. I've gone from there to hosting an event in London, a Developers Network in London – that's a journey."

Lloyd cites a favourite quote of his from Zig Ziglar: "'You don't have to be great to start; you just have to start, to be great.'

"Let's talk about that network meeting", Lloyd continues. "You've got the Developers Network that you host now, in conjunction with White Box. How can people get involved in that?"

"Yes, we host the Developers Network event in London, currently held at the Rocket Gallery, in Chelsea, a great venue", Fahd says. "It's held the second Wednesday of every month. If you just search online for Provident Homes, or the Developers Network, London, you'll find the links. And we're on Instagram, YouTube, Facebook, LinkedIn, etc.

"There are lots of other networking events out there," Fahd adds, "lots of other property events, but nothing like the one we do with White Box, which is specifically designed to help people transition into property. Our USP, our unique selling point, seems to be that we're working professionals who are managing to do this – we're full-time professionals outside of property. That's what we've been told. That's arguably one of the hardest transitions, because if you're already earning a decent income, and you're fully committed to your career after years of training, how do you jump ship into development?

So, we're attracting a lot of people in that situation. We wanted to create an event like this, because we struggled to find the right fit for us when we began networking. There are property events aimed for buy-to-let landlords, and there are exclusive developer clubs for really experienced developers, but we couldn't find anything in between, the steppingstone. We wanted to focus our attention on creating a learning environment, a supportive environment, and make it fun – what we call the White Box way."

"And it's going well", Lloyd notes. "It's really good. Anyone can attend that networking event for £25."

"It is a nice little community", Sreelal says, "where you can come every month and network with like-minded people."

"And that's how you started, isn't it?" Lloyd says. "At a networking event just like the London one. It's a great first step, a steppingstone as you said."

"That's how I met Fahd", Sreelal says. "It's definitely valuable, and everyone has something of value to add."

"The opportunities that come are ones you would never imagine, such as who you might meet. Sreelal and I are chalk and cheese – had it not been for that event that we attended, we would never have met each other. We are in entirely different circles, in different towns. We've got common ground now, but we would just not have intersected except for that networking session. What we identified though, after speaking a couple of times, were our complementary skill sets: my weaknesses were his strengths, and vice versa. People often make the mistake of working with people they're like, maybe who they're friends with, but too often they possess the same strengths, and the same weaknesses. That doesn't make for a balanced team.

"It was great to meet Sreelal", Fahd adds, "and learn of his credentials, his experience, and what skills he could add that I was missing. That's what's created a very powerful platform. And then Yelena joined us two years ago, and she's added to that as well. We call ourselves the tripod", he jokes.

"It is a great team you've got", Lloyd says. "The three of you really work well together. You can hear it in the banter between you, and see it in the way that you work."

"For anyone who wants to join us, just come, just be there. That's all. That's the beauty of network meetings. Just show up and rest will be taken care of."

"As we said, we're on Instagram, Facebook, etc. We've all got individual accounts, but you can also get in touch with us through our website, ProvidentHomes.co.uk.", Fahd adds. "We're looking forward to connecting with people, and really helping, sharing anything about our journey to help people along, even if it's just to show that it can be done. We're by no means the finished article. We've got a long, long road yet ahead of us, so, we know the challenges ahead. But I think we're relatable. People can see where we've come from in a short space of time. If that even just motivates people, that's great, because personal development has been a big part of our journey.

"That's something you guys at White Box practice and preach", Fahd says. "And we've seen you improve and progress in the years we've known you. Anything you learn, you pass straight back; you're not looking to filter or censor any information. You're very open and we see your trials as well as your tribulations.

"I've had people say to me that while we've done White Box training, there are other training courses out there, and they're anxious to pick the best one. I always tell them that some courses may be more detailed than White Box, some may offer more knowledge, but what I haven't seen or experienced in other courses, being honest here, is that you do not get the community – you don't get the support. Because what you guys at White Box offer is not limited to nine-to-five. Your doors are always open, and there's typically no time that's too inconvenient or a question that's too difficult to answer. You're always generally there to help. That's the real value. It's like a family of sorts – the Mastermind is like a family. The PDS, the Property Developers Secrets course, everyone greets each other like long-lost relatives! And the Facebook community – I don't know how you've managed to cultivate a community that has the same ethos that you preach, given there are over 20,000 people in that Facebook community, but it's a great privilege to be part of, well, a movement is what it feels like."

"It goes both ways", Lloyd says. "It's a privilege for us to be able help you and be part of your journey, as well as be friends. It's been amazing. Yeah, if you're looking for corporate, then we're not for you. We're not corporate, not a rigidly structured business. We're normal people, individuals, intent on helping normal people do amazing deals. Like the ones you guys are doing."

STEVE HAMMOND & SHANE TRAYNOR – NEW HOME COMPANY

www.newhomeco.uk

Instagram - @newhomecompanyuk

Shane - @thealrightinvestor

In this chapter we speak to Steve Hammond and Shane Traynor, from Birmingham. Steve is a very experienced builder and Shane is a very keen young lad who chose to initially learn the ropes of developments by helping Steve out. Shane participated in all of our online Developers Network events throughout lockdown, and when an opportunity arose, Shane jumped in, fully committed. He has helped Steve for a while now and the two of them work well together.

Steve was doing developments before joining White Box, but what Steve enjoys is the White Box community and the surrounding team, upon which he can call when need be. In property, it can be lonely if you try and do it all on your own. With White Box, however, that's not the case. You're never abandoned to do everything on your own.

"Welcome", Lloyd says, with a smile, "and thanks for joining the podcast. Let's start with you, Steve. Would you tell us a bit about your background, how you started property developments?"

"Sure", says Steve. "Initially, I went to university, then went and got a job, only to realise I didn't really want to work for anyone, but couldn't think of what I wanted to do. In the end,

I decided to set up a children's nursery for my wife to run. But to set up this nursery, I had to build it first.

"I took on a team of guys, we built the nursery, and I realized I quite enjoyed doing building work. So once the nursery was up and running, I decided to carry on doing building work. I did extensions, refurbs, renovations, and built up my own portfolio.

"But it's difficult to scale as a builder, to scale doing extensions and refurbs and things like that, so I decided to do development. At first, I did development on behalf of someone else, and he made a lot of money from it – but I didn't. That got me thinking this would be a good thing for me to do. So, after a quick break over the New Year, I decided to take a week off and go and buy a development.

"That first development was 14 apartments, and I finished that, but I stumbled a little bit because of COVID and had to go back to doing extensions. And since I had a little bit of time during lockdown, I started watching your YouTube videos and thought, well, it can't harm me to go on a weekend course. But I had absolutely no intention of joining the Mastermind at that point. I thought I would just learn a bit and that would be good. So, I went on the three-day PDS, the Property Developers Secrets course.

"What I didn't realize was that the biggest thing for me would be the network, the sharing of information. It's the potential joint ventures that you might get, the potential opportunities that the network might generate for you. And it was because of the calibre of people in the room that I decided to join the network. And because you only get out what you put in, I try to ensure that I am an active part of that.

"But, originally, you contacted me, Lloyd, and asked would I be interested in joining the Developers Network, and I said no, initially. We talked a bit more and you mentioned three other people who were interested in partnering, because I'd said I didn't want to do something on my own. You gave me their telephone numbers and I gave them each a call. Shane was one of them."

Lloyd smiles. "So, as you said, you stumbled into it, you kind of got the bug for it, you went for it, and you're going for it now, which is awesome. We recorded another podcast episode the other day that also emphasised the value of the network, where another developer realised he didn't have to do everything by himself – that you can't always do everything yourself. By partnering, co-venturing, you can build a business bigger and more quickly."

Steve nods. "Before this, I'd always done everything myself, figured out how to do something and worked it all out for myself. Luckily, that's mostly worked out for me. It's interesting, though, how much I've learned over the past 12 months, not just about development but about funding, about business, about lots of different investment strategies, and how to organize and manage it all. It takes a lot to figure that out for yourself, whereas if you can jump on to education or networking with knowledgeable people who can shortcut some of that for you, you can really save a lot of time and effort. You've got to be prepared to make mistakes, and figure things out as you go, but you also can save yourself time by listening to what other experienced people are doing."

"I agree", says Andi. "You've clearly gone through this taking a more practical route, like I did. I came up through carpentry, and then built my own small building company, a similar story to yours. Arguably, some people think that the Property Developer Secrets training course is about teaching people the practical side of how to build houses, but it's more about how to put a skilled team together that can build houses and manage the project. You have a certain skill set, the practical side of it, but, as you say, other people possess other skill sets. You don't have to learn everything – you don't have to know everything – you just have to put a good team together to cover all the bases."

"I think that is true", Steve says. "In fact, understanding the more granular aspects of building can have its downsides, because you can't help but meddle. If your role was strictly as a professional developer, someone handling the administrative side of things, you wouldn't involve yourself with how the taps are going to be connected, or how the wall is going to be built. For me, because I've got the background in building and what's involved, I can't help but get involved in it. Admittedly, I think that enables us to get a better-quality outcome, and this is why, I feel, that we're doing the barn conversions. I feel they're more in line with what we should be doing, because I genuinely think we can be among the best high-end builders and developers. I don't think we would be the best at making smaller 'boxes'. Our quality is high, but our efficiency isn't quite as high as you might need in smaller builds, if that makes sense."

"And with the barn conversions you mentioned", Lloyd says, "you sold one for over asking, more than you advertised it for, which is impressive. And you have another one, which you're also selling?"

Steve nods. "We've only had it on for a couple of weeks. I'm pleased that we got the first one done; it's a very niche product – they're two large agricultural barns. With them, we're celebrating the industrial agricultural look, so we're featuring anthracite, concrete, metals, marble, and wood, so they're quite contemporary; they're not your stereotypical lots-of-beams-on-show sort of stuff.

"So, it's more niche market. And then, hopefully, we'll have some more lined up shortly. Hopefully, we'll sell this second one within the next few weeks. And, actually, it's been really good. We got a lot more profit than we'd anticipated. It's cost us a lot more than I ever would have thought, but because they're unique, we're able to sell them for more than we thought.

"The agents told us that the most expensive house in the whole of South Birmingham was £491 per square foot. If we had priced them at £750,000, that would have come out to £500 per square foot. But because we went for £795,000", Steve says, grinning, "which was something like £565 per square foot, we have absolutely smashed the ceiling for the whole of South Birmingham."

"It just goes to show that when you provide quality, people are willing to pay for it", Lloyd says. "So, let's hear from Shane now. Shane, tell us your story of how and where you started and how you met Steve and decided to partner."

"Well, looking back to 2020", Shane says, "I was travelling around New Zealand when the first lockdown took place, and I was trying to figure out what I wanted to do when I got home. Originally, I was in the music industry, but I didn't really like it, didn't really get on with the types of people in that industry, and so I wanted a bit of a change, but wasn't sure what I wanted to do. I knew I needed to figure out a way to grow my wealth over time, to create financial security, because of what was happening with COVID." He chuckles. "Honestly, I didn't even know what a mortgage was, back in mid-2020. I didn't have a clue!"

"Not exactly what we're taught in school, is it?" Lloyd says, shaking his head. "I learned what a mortgage was by playing Monopoly, not through my education. Strange."

"Yes, even credit card debt and things like that don't get taught in school", Shane says. "I just started watching YouTube videos on how to get wealthy, to find out what types of books to read. Up until then, I think I'd read two books in my life: one was a Goosebumps book, and the other was half a James Bond novel", he says, laughing. "I went to a used bookstore in New Zealand and picked up the typical ones: Rich Dad, Poor Dad; Think and Grow Rich; How to Win Friends and Influence People – those sorts of books. I. didn't think I'd learn all that much just by doing that, but I did learn a lot, and now I love reading books. I read about what vehicles would help me to get wealthy over time and give something to the world, and one of the vehicles is property.

"So, I started YouTubing property and found that I liked the idea of development. I thought buy-to-lets seemed good, a good stepping stone, but there are a lot of people in them at the moment and they're kind of slow. And then I came across White Box, one of your videos, something like 'Property Millionaire by 30', or something, and I was intrigued by it. I've since watched more of your videos, and was impressed at how you include a lot of educational content. And that made me think: I want to be a property developer.

"Then I read your book, and learned a lot from that, but began to wonder how could I be a property developer without much knowledge, zero experience, and no money, because I've just blown it all on travelling.

"I flew home in August 2020 and started participating in the weekly White Box Wednesday Zoom calls, and through those, I met loads of good people, and learned loads. I think it was that November or December, Lloyd, when you announced you were going to hold a networking event in the New Year and you were looking to do it in Birmingham."

"It was September", Lloyd recalls. "I don't think you could have been on the network for that long by then, if you joined in August. That was just coming to the end of lockdown. Around March 2020, every single Wednesday we jumped online and gave some content away. It was more to help keep spirits up – that was really the main reason we started doing the Zoom calls, because lockdown was tough for a lot of people. We just wanted to maintain some regular contacts, which became the start of the Developers Network. We wanted to make these meetings localised, to bring them to different areas of the UK. Birmingham was one of the areas we targeted, and you were one of the first to put your name in the hat."

"I remember that", Andi says. "You joined in August, you showed up every week, you had your camera on every week, whereas a lot of people chose to just sit silently, in the background. Whilst you may, inside, have felt a bit of imposter syndrome diving into a world you weren't familiar with, you got yourself out there, you interacted, you voiced questions, all a part of being in the network. You personify that saying I often quote: 'Activity creates opportunity'. You've been active. You've read books, you got out there, you participated in events."

Shane nods. "You hit the nail on the head when you mentioned I was probably suffering a bit of imposter syndrome. It definitely felt like that, but instead of thinking that I couldn't do the network because I'm not a developer, I thought, why not just ask the question?

"So, I messaged Lloyd and asked, 'Can I do this network even though I've got no experience?' and, to my surprise, he suggested we chat, which we did, and at the end he said I could do it, however, I needed to do it with someone who had experience. That wasn't an outright no, so I just had to find a developer who would do it with me. I called up a couple of people that I knew locally, and then Steve rang me on a Friday night during dinner, and he quizzed me fairly intensively as to why I wanted to join the network, why I want to get into developments, I guess to make sure I was motivated, that I wasn't going to attend one session and then abandon it."

"We definitely want the network meetings to be educational, valuable, to all participants. The reason we say to joint venture with someone with experience in developing is because we want the people who host to have knowledge to share. And doing a joint venture with someone experienced will get you experience and open up opportunities for further joint ventures."

"So, Steve and I eventually met up", Shane explains, "at that barn conversion that Steve mentioned earlier. We talked for over three hours, and he said, 'Look, I need someone to help me find land for future developments, to help me grow the business, and free up some of my time. You want to quit your job?' Shane chuckles. "I was working at school as an IT technician, not really doing what I wanted to. It took me just 24 hours to decide. I spoke to a few trusted people in my circle, but although I'd never been self-employed before, it was a no brainer, to be honest. And the best decision I've ever made.

"So, Steve and I started the network. We've done four events now, as of January 2022, and just as a result of that, one of the biggest land and new homes commercial agents in Birmingham, West Midlands, approached me on LinkedIn saying they'd like to meet with us and send us off-market opportunities – just from holding this networking event! We're not worried now, are we, Steve, about getting money for our next developments? That's not even an issue for us.

"Instead, I'm struggling to find enough time to evaluate all the off-market deals coming to us! Now, not all of them stack up, of course, but the point I want to make is that all this is stemming solely from our doing this networking event alone! It has absolutely propelled us in terms of opportunity, skills, and our network."

Steve nods. "The joint venture has really helped both of us. As an individual, you rarely bring everything you need to the table on your own. But the two of us together have benefited each other. I had the building experience, and some financial knowledge, I had some investors, I had some opportunities. But I couldn't manage it all. Shane focuses his time and attention on exploiting and growing all of that, which I couldn't do.

"A business owner has to spin a lot of plates. There are only so many plates you can spin, and I was spinning way too many, and way too many were dropping. The benefit in this for Shane is that he gets to be a developer without needing to have money to invest in it, initially, so he's gaining credibility, a network, knowledge, contacts, links, and experience. That's what I saw that first night we talked, that here was someone who was going to give it his all – he might not know everything, but he's going to have a go. So", he adds, laughing, "Shane will get a phone call from me at 10 pm, when I'm still working, because I know he's still working."

"And I'm sure that would not have been an easy decision for you, Steve", says Lloyd. "We've known each other for a while now, and I'm sure you were wondering whether to bring Shane on, or talk to him in the first place, given his inexperience, unsure whether he might be the right person. Shane said you'd grilled him a bit, asking him a load of questions to figure out whether he was the right person to partner with. In hindsight though, seeing what you are both doing and how you're helping each other, I'm sure you'd agree it was a great decision."

"I do", Steve says. "I think it's benefited both of us. And going back to the subject of the networking events that Shane said helped him, I'd say it's one of the best moves I've made as well. You could argue that the events have detracted from the number of opportunities I've been able to look at, and the builds that I've been able to do, but it has helped me to get back on track."

"Yes, more opportunities will come later", Lloyd says.

"I was trying too hard to do everything all by myself", Steve admits. "The White Box Portugal retreat that I did with you guys made me realise that I had to scale back, because all I was doing was just keeping people busy. So, I took some opportunities along the way to reduce my team, and that has had a knock-on effect on how much work we can take on. Now, I've got to start building that back up, through the subcontract approach, although that's always a challenge, because you got to manage quality as well, which is easier when it's all your business."

"Yes, we talked about the structural ways in which your business was built", Andi recalls, "which weren't helping, so like you said, you needed to retract a little bit in order to build back in another way that was both busy and profitable, where you could add more projects to the hopper and expand in the right way."

"The Developers Network", Steve says, "is bringing in stuff that we could never have imagined. We had people at the last event asking if we'd be interested in being a part of their business. One guy even said, 'You should organize a golfing holiday, because I think people would pay to spend time with you'." He chuckles. "I couldn't have imagined anything like that a year ago!"

"In terms of our goal of how to help people get started", Lloyd says, "have you any words of advice or tips you can give people who are thinking about getting into developments, perhaps someone who's in the trade who's looking to take that next step?"

"Whenever people ask me that sort of question", Steve says, "I always suggest that they figure out what they have that other people need. For me, because I had the build ability – I had the build team – and I had the financial knowledge, but I didn't have as much money to draw on as I would have liked. That told me I had to link myself with money first, to link myself with opportunity.

"I've had people with money say to me, 'I'd like to become a developer'", Steve says. "And my response is invariably, 'Well, you've got the money already, so why don't you become a professional investor in development instead, rather than trying to learn how to be a builder?' So, my advice is to figure out what it is you're good at within this realm, stick to that, and gather other people around you who are good at the things you're not. You can't be the best at all of it, so stick to what you can be the best at and build a solid team around you."

"What about you, Shane?" Lloyd asks.

"Well, I'd like to share a bit about where I am at the moment, a bit of progress I'm making. At the last development network event, I approached a lending company, and said, 'Now that you know that I'm working with Steve, how long do I have to wait now to do my first development for myself? Is it another year of experience? Two years?' And he said, 'Shane, because you're doing this network, because you know Steve, you know architecture, you know planners, and you have all of these networks of people around you now, all you need is just the deposit for the plot of land and we'll give you the rest.'

"I was astonished", Shane admitted. "But while I wasn't in a position to start then, that's a prime example of what this community can do for you. So, my advice to people in my position who would like to get into development when they have no money, no experience, and no practical knowledge is to just believe you can do it – don't be close-minded. Network your absolute ass off, go to these events, like the Developer's Network, and if you want to learn developments from it, find a developer who will take you under their wing. That's how I found Steve. I've met two other people, a guy from London who's my age and another guy, Lewis, who's part of the network, who did the exact same thing, with no experience, money, or knowledge and now they're each doing developments. I believe that if you just project what you want into the world, the world will give you what you want."

"Solid advice there", Lloyd says, "and you've made some great progress. Shane, as you said, you asked the questions and you got your answers, but if you don't ask the questions, you won't find out the answers. So, credit to you for asking the questions. And, Steve, I think yours is also great advice, about doing what you're good at. And so many people mistakenly think that what they're doing now is not relevant to what they want to do in development, but there actually there are a lot of transferable skills, as you can attest to."

"To build on what Shane's just said", Steve adds, "if you're someone who's in Shane's position, my advice is to put yourself out there and offer your services to a more experienced person at a lower rate – that's you investing in yourself. Think of it as an apprenticeship of sorts. Be willing to work for significantly less at first in order to add value. If you remove the risk from the person who's willing to consider taking you on, the learning you get in return will be well worth the wages you might sacrifice initially.

"Once you start bringing value to that person, your wages will go up. More importantly, Shane is now moving in circles as a developer, and people won't even be aware that he might still be learning – he'll be doing, because he can draw on and share his experience with the barn conversions we're doing.

"In fact, we're about to complete an exchange Friday on a house that Shane found. He'll be able to say, 'I found that, and I was involved in designing what we're going to do with it, defining the plan for it, working out who we're going to rent it to, how much work we're going to do', etc. If I had done what Shane's done 20 years ago, I'd be significantly further on than I am now, because I mistakenly tried to do it all myself."

"From our perspective", Andi says, "watching this process happening, there's been tremendous respect exhibited towards each other. You could have easily brushed Shane off, Steve, because he had no experience, and told him instead, 'I'm not interested.' And, Shane, you might not have even approached Steve, because he was so much further along. But you both put yourself out there, you've each been willing to make yourself vulnerable, which is a key point, I think, and shown each other a lot of respect." Andi chuckles. "It's been a bit of a bromance in our eyes, looking on it from the outside."

Laughter

"Seriously though", Andi adds, "that's been really good to see. I don't think a lot of people are willing or brave enough to open up and put themselves into that vulnerable position – on both sides – to let that flourish. It's not an overnight thing; you have to build that relationship. All developments, all properties, are predicated on relationships. It's been a great process to watch."

"Looking forward to the next chapter," Lloyd says, adding, "I don't mean in the book, but in your world."

Laughter

"Well", Shane says, "we might just write a book as well!"

KEVIN MOULTON & CRAIG ROBERTS – DWELLINGS 4 U

http://www.dwellings4u.co.uk/

Kevin Moulton and Craig Roberts are longstanding clients of White Box, but it all started with an impromptu meeting in our office. Kevin and Craig had attended the network event that we used to run in Northampton, after deciding they wanted to do something different, professionally. They were both from the trades background, with Kevin owning and running a plumbing company and Craig being hands on as a brickie. They knew what went on, on sites, but they didn't know how to do it for themselves, so they did some research and discovered White Box Property Solutions. During that initial meeting, Andi invited them to the pub afterwards, to continue to conversation. That meeting filled Kevin and Craig with so much confidence that we were the right people to educate and mentor them. That was back in 2017. We still mentor them to date…

"Welcome, Kevin and Craig, to the podcast, and to the book Building the Dream", Lloyd begins. "Let's talk about the dream you're currently on, what you're doing right now, and then we'll go back to the beginning, where it all started for you."

"Well, currently, we're on our Tower Court project, about our biggest one to date", says Craig. The reason we love this project, just to give you a quick overview, is that it was seven commercial units, some of them with tenants and some of them vacant. It also came with a large car park that had planning to build five terraced houses.

"We purchased this quite a bit below market value", Craig adds, "and using what you taught us, we used prior approval (because the first floor was all offices) to get four apartments, and we're now in the planning system to see if we can add an extra storey for another four. Eight apartments in total, so an uplift of the commercial buildings, plus five new builds in the carpark."

"What sort of GDV are you looking at?" Lloyd asks. (GDV stands for gross development value, which is the total value the property will be worth once the project is completed.)

"For the new builds, the five houses", Craig says, "we're looking at £1.3–1.4 million, and the commercial portion is £570,000. The eight apartments add just over another £1 million GDV, so we're looking at about £3.7 million GDV for the entire project."

"That's brilliant", Lloyd says. "But this isn't your first deal in the area, is it? Just down the road – maybe 300 metres? – you completed your first site since joining us. So, you tested this first on a smaller project, one that was only six flats, part conversion, part new build?"

Kevin nods. "When we purchased the site, we were meant to knock about half of it down and add a couple of new builds on the end of it to convert it into six houses. But then the structural engineer asked, 'Why are you knocking that half down when this half is in just as bad a state?' That was quite a plus, really, because it saved quite a lot of build costs, although we did have to put a fair bit of steel back into the build. It was a fantastic end project, and certainly very hairy along the way.

After that, we both said, 'If we can do this, and we can do anything'."

"Absolutely", Lloyd concurs. "So, the area that you guys are working in is the east coast, the east side of the UK, and now you're on your second project, with a power team around you as well. I think having the power team around you is quite key for you guys."

Kevin nods. "Definitely. And knowing your area well is something that you and Andi always reinforced for us: 'Learn your area', you'd say, over and over.

"I think a lot of people look into doing these kinds of deals do so thinking they'll target a popular investment area, but not one they actually know. The best place to do development is where you live", Kevin adds, "the area you know. You do hear about someone doing well in a certain area, but I think every strategy works; it's more about finding the one that's best suited to your area, not someone else's."

"So", Lloyd prompts, "tell us how you each started, what your background is. You were both in the trades, I know, but that didn't mean that you necessarily knew how to do developments, did it?"

"I think when you speak to people", Craig says, "a lot of our journeys started the same way. I had listened to the audio book Rich Dad, Poor Dad. And as a self-employed bricklayer, I found myself wanting to do more. I wanted more in my life, more for my family's life. That's when I approached Kevin, because he was quite successful at the time, building up his plumbing company, and both of us wanted to get into property."

Kevin nods. "I remember it well. Craig came over and

encouraged me to come with him to this one-day course to see if I was interested. As Craig said, I'd built up a plumbing company from scratch to turning over £2.3 million or so at the time, pre-COVID days. So, we went along to that course."

"That course mainly centred on the buy–refurbish–refinance model", Craig notes. "We both mainly did our work in new builds and we wanted to build stuff, we knew how to build stuff, we had our own trades, we have the connections and know the trades to use. Our next step was to put all the pieces together so we could get started with our own developments."

"And, also", Kevin says, "speaking for myself, before this, I worked mainly with big developers, and I'm not going to lie – it was a struggle with them, because the ball is always in their court. I had to rely on them to pay me. And something that Craig is really passionate about, as he said, is setting up a legacy for our families. And we're not going to do that working for somebody else. So, even though I had my own company, which was turning over good money, we were still working for and relying on others for our success."

Lloyd nods. "I know that both of you are big family guys, and family means everything to you. This is called 'Building the Dream', and the dream for you two was to build for yourself, rather than building for other people, being contracted to work on other people's sites.

"I don't know any other bricklayers who would be listening to a self-improvement audiobook instead of just bantering with everyone around them", Lloyd says. "That's something different right there. You identified your passion and managed to insert working on it into what you were doing. You demonstrated the passion for learning early on, which is great, and you were eager to take the next step. So, what are the next steps for you? What's next?"

"From that course, we decided that we wanted to get started with the buy–refurbish–refinance model, before deciding that we wanted to build", Craig explains. "So, we start asking around, and that was the time that you and Andi were hosting your network event in Northampton. I came down to meet you guys. At the time, we were really keen to get started. We'd found a site, we'd spoken to a few investors to secure funding, but we just didn't know how it would all work, and you were kind enough to invite us over to the office for a chat."

"When you first came to White Box, to the network meeting we'd been running since about 2015", Lloyd says, "you approached us afterwards and said, 'Look, could we just have a bit of your time? Could we come to the office, as we've got some ideas – we want to do something but we're not really sure where and how to start.' That's something we're always happy to do for people.

"I remember the four of us sitting around this very desk I'm seated at now", he adds, "and you gave Andi and me some background on what you were doing, said you'd been on the one-day course and had the drive, the hunger, to do something more. And although I was busy that evening, Andi continued the meeting in the pub, afterwards." He chuckles.

Craig smiles. "I remember it clearly. We went out for dinner with Andi. As you know, I've a perpetual thirst for knowledge and, like you said, I was bricklaying and listening to audiobooks, not joining in with the chitchat. I wanted to learn more, to learn ways to improve my life. And when I shared that with

Andi, it turned out he was also into audiobooks. And when Kevin mentioned that he was going to Cheltenham, because Kevin's a big fan of the horses, Andi turned to him and said, 'The horse you want to be backing is this one', pointing to me. There and then, we made the decision to do a deal. I agreed to come along on the three-day course, and it went from there, really."

"The education part is something that not everyone gets", Lloyd notes. "Our advice at the time, if you recall, because our mission is to help people get results, was to just do the three-day course and go from there. We weren't telling you to do anything more than that, but to take that important first step and learn first. Then, if you liked what you heard, what you learned, and you still wanted to do it, that's when you'd move forward, to the next level. Tell us, what did you think about the three-day course? You definitely had the drive to start by getting an education first, but was it a challenge for you to go and do that, initially?"

"It wasn't a challenge to do the three-day course, if that's what you're asking", Craig says. "We just clicked with it straightaway. We were looking forward to it, as we'd both decided that this was the path we might want to take. We were excited to start, and it just went on, leaps and bounds, from there.

"For some, to part with what the course costs might make them hesitate – it is a considerable amount of money to some people – but that said, a lot of them would blow that same amount of money on a holiday or something, that has no return beyond the memory of a good time", Craig points out. "In contrast, the money we spent on those three days has returned to us tenfold – at least! From there, we elected to continue on to your Mastermind course, because we believed it was important for us to get support along the way, because it is challenging. I wouldn't sit here and say it's easy to do development – we're challenged every day – but it's all a part of it. That's what makes it more enjoyable, the more challenging, the more enjoyable it is at the end, when you've achieved it."

"Absolutely", Lloyd says, nodding. "So, if you're living the dream now, what rewards have you experienced now that you've taken that step and done your own developments?"

"Going to Bali, for one!" Craig exclaims.

Laughter

"Going back to family", Kevin says, "it's what we're creating." He glances up at the nearby whiteboard displaying the project's financials. "I'm looking at these numbers at the moment, always with an eye to see where we could improve, because things can go wrong. Doing developments is not easy, like Craig said. The main driver for us is to build the dream to create something for our kids and grandkids to have. I can walk by something we've done with my grandkids, point to it, and say, proudly, 'Gramps did that!'"

"At the moment", Craig adds, "this project brings in a gross income of £54,000 a year and knowing that, as the housing market increasing, that portfolio of what's now only six houses is increasing at the same time, and that will be there to pass on to our children. We've also got our own dreams, in this moment, our own goals that we want to achieve. One of mine was to send my children to private school. The upbringing I had, I didn't have those opportunities, and now, come September 2022, my eldest is going to a grammar school, so it is moving towards giving us the life we want. Obviously, everyone's vision, everyone's dream of what they want, is different, but for us, doing developments is enabling us to achieve those things."

"A perfect example of that", Kevin says, "is that on Tuesday I'm flying out to South Africa for three weeks".

"I remember a defining moment for you, Kevin", Lloyd says. "You were talking about your running your plumbing business simultaneously – we talked about it a lot, but in that initial Mastermind session Craig mentioned earlier, I sensed there was a bit of a mindset block in you regarding what you were doing. You were trying to do developments, but you were still running your plumbing business, so your focus was split. There was one piece of advice that we gave you that changed things for you, to think only in terms of: Let's focus on developments. Do you recall that?"

"Yes", Kevin says. "Now, my view is that I own a plumbing and heating company, but I run a development company. Back then I didn't have any office staff at the plumbing and heating business; I did everything myself, which presented its own set of challenges. That's all changed now. It's created bigger overhead, but we're making it work now. For example, I've got an estimator now, I've got Sue, who runs the office, we've got a contracts man, Joe, who looks after the blokes, and I'm just called in when I'm needed, which is great. We've got an FD as well. So, we slowly built all of that up since White Box. You're right, that was a major mindset change."

"I remember the first time you joined us in Bali", Lloyd says. "Your concentration was divided. You were trying to sort your plumbing business out while you were abroad. But the second time you came to Bali, the year after, and you were a different bloke, focused. You weren't running around like a headless chicken. You were looking after yourself and what you wanted to gain on that retreat, and the business was running itself back home, without you."

Kevin nods. "That was a big mindset change, without a doubt. But now it runs itself. I've got good people in there looking after that side of things, like Mark, who's been with me since the start. He's moved up, further and further. He wants to hoist me out, I think!"

Laughter

"What I like about you guys", Lloyd says, "is that you throw yourself at everything, fully committed. We teach people to copy what we do, because what we've done has worked for us, the idea being that since we've been through a few deals, we don't try and change things, because we know now what works and what doesn't, what's good and what's bad. But you guys took it literally", Lloyd says, laughing. "The first deal Andi and I ever did was called St James. What's the name of your first deal?"

Craig grins. "St James!"

"Our office here is called Tower Court", Lloyd adds. "What's the name of the project you're working on now?"

"Tower Court", Kevin says, laughing.

"You guys really do throw yourself fully at everything", Lloyd says, admiringly. "You now run the Cambridge Developers Network, which is a part of the White Box Developers Network programme. You love networking, you love meeting people, and you're great at building up a team around you, which I'm convinced has been one key to your success."

"We do love helping people as well", Craig says. "That was what the networking was all about. We launched the first-ever network with White Box, as that was really our vision: to help others in the way that we were helped. We believe that if you can pass something on, even if it's just a little bit of knowledge, or help someone in some way, you are giving back by helping someone else achieve their goals."

Kevin nods. "The network evenings have been great, and we're now starting to build again, post-pandemic. We're getting quite a little family within our network evenings as well. People are starting to connect with each other more, starting to work with each other, becoming more informed, more educated. It's just brilliant to see that, really."

"We'll discuss what advice you'd give to others starting out, or thinking about getting started, but first I want to ask you about profit. What's the profit shaping up to be on the deal you're working on now, Tower Court?"

"Some of the elements are in planning. We're looking at a new build at the back, which we should make about a £300,000 profit from. If we get the planning for the extra storey, because the land has already been purchased and we bought that well below market value, we estimate making up to about £1.5 million profit."

Lloyd shakes his head in admiration. "That's really incredible. I know there's a lot to go yet, but, still, that's impressive."

"It can be difficult to predict these profits", Kevin admits.

Craig adds, "And that's in a perfect world, where we don't hit any roadblocks. Well", he adds, correcting himself, "I should say that's in an achievable world. There are always going to be obstacles, whether that ends up being the case here, but to reflect now on where we were at before we started this road versus where we are now... Sometimes I don't think we're enough aware of how far we've come. We're so busy in the present, throwing ourselves into everything", he adds, shaking his head, "that we don't take a moment to reflect on how far we've come, where we're at now versus where we were when we started."

"I think that's common", Lloyd notes. "I think a lot of people focus on where they're going, but not necessarily on how far they've come. It's important to look back, to reflect on what you've learned throughout the process, and it's rewarding to do it, to congratulate yourself and say, 'I really have come a long way.' It can make the journey forward that little bit easier, having reflected on what you've accomplished thus far."

"We all have our favourite sayings", Craig says, "and one of mine is 'Stand still and you go backwards.' But yes, if it does all go well, in two or three years' time, it will be helpful to really look back on it all."

Kevin adds, "I think a core important thing, when it comes to developments, or any property strategy, is buying well. Using Tower Court as an example, when the valuation came in, we'd already made £285,000 because we got it at below market value. That advantage right at the start gave us that buffer for any mishaps or mistakes we might encounter along the way."

"And you'd been through a few sites", Lloyd notes, "and made a few offers, so it's not like this all came from the first deal you ever looked at. You had to invest some time into the process before you found that site."

"If there's one thing I'd tell anyone starting out", Craig says, "it's that it's hard to get started. You've got to be offering on everything and building those relationships with landowners, with estate agents..."

"With investors", Kevin adds.

"Yes, investors", Craig agrees. "It's really hard to get started, but now, after that initial investment of time and effort, we've got a bit of history, we've got a bit of traction now, and so it is getting easier."

"That's what you and Andi always reminded us, that the first one is always the hardest", Kevin says.

"It's the whole riding-the-bike analogy", Lloyd adds. "To get started, you've got to put some momentum and effort into turning the pedals. You can then change gear, and when you've got better, and are in the higher gear, it becomes easier, you pick up momentum. It's much easier once you've got momentum, but you've got to get started first, which takes considerably more effort.

"Talking about getting started", he adds, "many of our readers might be on the fence, just thinking about getting started, or maybe they're ready to start or upscale into property, so what kind of advice would you offer them?"

"Just do something – take action. There are a lot of people who spend considerable money on property courses, and not just in property, but they hesitate. The ones who achieve success are the ones who commit to moving forward, who throw themselves into it and take action. I don't mean doing anything impulsively, but get started, learn the market, start making offers. The ones who hesitate, who don't do anything because they're over-thinking it – it's analysis paralysis. Those are the ones who never go anywhere and yet, with all the courses they keep taking, they probably know more than us!"

Kevin nods. "One example of what Craig's talking about, looking back at our first project, St James Street, there was one point where, if there had been a heavy wind, that building would have fallen over. It was that scary. Just standing inside made me think, 'Oh, my God...' If I'd known that beforehand, before I'd ever taken the course, I probably wouldn't have moved forward on it. So, going back to what Craig said about education, going for it, but sticking to the golden rule to buy right can give you the cushion you need to get it all done. Another deal, an iron in the fire we can't talk specifics on right now, has fantastic numbers, and we have a good sense of where we can take it, because of the education we got with White Box."

"The right education", Lloyd says, with a smile. "As Andi likes to say, 'Action creates opportunity'. Well, it's been a pleasure to share your journey with you, and of course we're still working with you, still helping you along your process, as we've done the past three years."

"It's been a great three years, mate", Kevin says.

"Through all of the ups and downs, you've always been there to support us and we appreciate that", Craig adds.

"Absolutely", Kevin says. "A point I'd really like to stress is that every time we pick the phone up, you've always been there, whenever."

Lloyd smiles. "That's who we are!"

NEIL BRIGGS – INSPIRED

In this chapter we talk to Neil Briggs, who is fairly local to us, in Milton Keynes. Neil first attended the Property Developers Secrets course in 2016. Neil jumped into action straight away and was soon admiringly nicknamed Neil 'The Deal' Briggs. He managed to pick up a few developments to start with, from one house to four or five.

One particular site, called Simpson, was a joint venture with us. Neil found this plot on the market and asked if we would joint venture with him on the development. As it was local and we had the capacity to take it on, we did. It certainly had its challenges along the way, but it's a development site that we are very proud of, to this day. Neil continues to develop and work with others too. Neil also has a great eye for spotting a deal and has started sourcing deals for other people as well.

"Today", Andi says, "we're talking to Neil Briggs, who was on one of our first Property Developers Secrets course. Neil, give us a rundown of what you were doing before you got into developments, why you chose to come on White Box's Property Developers Secrets course back in 2015, and then we'll talk about what you've done since."

"I was in property already, before the course", Neil says. "I started as a financial advisor in mortgages in 2001, and that grew to where I set up my own estate agency in 2010, which is still operating. I had bought and sold a few properties, including a house with a large garden, which led me to White Box, as the idea was to build another unit on it, maybe a bungalow. But I didn't know much about building houses, although I knew quite a lot about property, property finance, buying and selling, and flipping. Yours is the only training course I've ever done. Obviously, being in the industry, I didn't need to learn how to buy a house, but doing the building itself was new territory for me. I have done a few refurbs though, and had a good team of guys I was working with. So, the next stage was to find out the process of going through planning, and the build process for a new dwelling. I searched the internet, started chatting with Lloyd online, and booked into the Property Developers Secrets two-day course, as it was back then, at the Northampton Hilton."

Lloyd smiles. "I remember. Funnily enough, we held it in the very same room as the auction site where we purchased our first property, the first ever deal we did when we were getting started. So, we've followed you for a long time now."

"And we're now business partners as well", Neil adds, "as we've done a few deals together, personally. That's a good part of being in the White Box community. You get people involved, people who are like-minded, and share the same goals for success. People who were on the same course as me ultimately did some joint ventures together, and I still see some of the people who were on that course. Everyone takes it to their own level in terms of how they want to do developments. Some people never take the next step, but others make a success of it. I'm very much all or nothing, so I give things my all, but I really love doing the developments and feel I've found my niche."

"Obviously there's a big list", Lloyd says, "but tell us what sort of deals you've done since doing the two-day course."

"Well, we started with the single let with a large garden I

mentioned earlier", Neil says, "but we sold that on, as we didn't get planning on it because it was too small for what we wanted to do. And, as mentioned, we've done some projects together, you and I. I already had a shop in Rush and High Streets when I signed up for the course, and that course changed my thinking. I converted a two-bedroom flat into a five-bedroom HMO, a conversion that Red Box did for me at the time.

"Then I bought a shop across the road, which I've since converted into four flats and two shops, then bought the shop next door to do the same – four flats and two shops – and I'm just finishing one in Newport Pagnell now, which is three flats and two shops. In addition, I'm in for planning for a 15-unit scheme at the moment, in Kettering, on Montagu Street, which has planning for 10 but I'm trying to get 15. And I've got a nine-bed HMO on that road as well, which, again, we worked with Red Box on.

"And I've built a couple of bungalows with someone I met on the Mastermind, did a site in Hereford, which didn't go as well as planned. I've got Newport Pagnell, the house I'm living in now, which was initially going to be sold and now I'm buying it with a joint venture partner.

"I've got stuff in planning, Newport PagnellNewport Pagnell with two units, and I'm looking at a massive site at the moment. I've retained a lot of my units, instead of trying to sell many of them. My sweet spot has been working with retail and permitted development rights, and retaining the retail. I've got a couple in Milton Keynes, and a couple in Northamptonshire that are finished.

"That's about it, I think. I lose track and forget how many

properties I've got, to be honest. I list them on a spreadsheet." Neil chuckles. "It's a nice problem to have!"

"I think we've run out of time!" Lloyd jokes. "You've done a heck of a lot since that two-day course!"

"What's key here to me", Andi says, "is that the first property you came on the course for, adding that bungalow, didn't work in the end. We see this quite a lot, where building one house isn't always cost effective. But you learned the process, you learned how to scale up, you learned how to focus your strategy on shops and uppers and things like that. You needed to go through the course to get to that point, and as soon as you found your niche, you rolled it out."

"Absolutely. I must have done 10 retail conversions by now, and I've done an office-to-residential conversion, which my business partner bought me out of. I'm always adaptable, open to change. In this game, it is always about finding a solution. One of the first sites that I bought, again on a high street, I rushed in, assuming I would get planning on it, no problem. Instead, it's taken two or three years to get the planning permission, because the council didn't like what I was proposing. I've won three planning appeals so far on that building. That was a purchase of a shop with a flat above, and I've currently got four flats above and two retail on the ground floor, with potentially another unit out the back at the storage shed. That was a purchase price of £175,000 and when I refinanced it, it was valued at nearly £700,000. So, I paid a lot of interest in bridging loans due to the delays, and so I reckon it was an expensive lesson to learn, but what I've learned through the planning process of that has helped with my other sites."

"I think the key is to have long-term vision", Andi says. "What we hear in all of these interviews is the desire to be a developer for life. We don't want to just do a one-off and that's it. You take the lessons you learn and implement them all in every subsequent project. That's where the real value is."

Neil nods. "You only fail when you stop. I've had success with every single site, but every site has come with its own particular problems. There was one development we did where we lost a lot of money because of the default interest, the build cost went up, and it was kind of out of my area, which taught me that I need to be more in control, stay local. When you're too far away, it's harder to keep your finger on the pulse of what's happening. So, I've since created a few rules for myself, such as I won't travel any more than an hour to a site, because of the loss of productivity the travel generates. If I'm back within an hour, I then have time to accomplish other things that day. Activity creates opportunity, Andi – isn't that what you always say?"

"Absolutely", Andi says. "That's 100% it."

"Not every deal goes as planned", Lloyd affirms. "In fact, I'd say that every deal one does strays in some way from the initial plan. If you think it's going to go smoothly, that's not going to be the case. Developments will be challenging; they will, at times, be tough; there will be things that go wrong, but it's all about how you overcome them. You said, yourself, that every problem has a solution, and I agree. You only fail if and when you stop; it's never a failure if you keep moving forward. It is simply a learning curve that we all have to confront. I think it's smart to stick to your local area, to stick to within an hour of your base location. So", he adds, "for anyone who's thinking of getting into this, do you have any particular advice for them?"

Neil considers the question. "I'd recommend against getting too fixed on a specific type and size of project in your head. When I first started, I decided to join the Mastermind to give me a level of accountability I didn't previously have in my work. I was running my own firm at the time, and I was the one making the decisions. I didn't have to account to anyone else for the decisions I made. The Mastermind, however, gave me that monthly accountability. But because I had a rigidly fixed idea of the type and size project I wanted to do, it took a good six months for me to actually get something over the line. At that point, I had changed that fixed mindset of wanting X number of units and focused more on just ensuring that each project could generate a good return. Once I allowed myself that flexibility, I found the site that we did a joint venture on together, I found a lot of other sites, and things started to fall more into place. What I had originally envisioned, a certain number of units in my area with planning permission, turned out to be few and far between.

"So, in terms of what I would say to people wanting to start out is: Network as much as you can – speak to the people who have been around the scene and learn from what they've done – but you must take action. So many times I see people who have done the courses five or six years earlier and asked them what they've done and it turns out they haven't taken action, not so much as on a single let, solely out of fear of taking that first step. So, I would encourage people to start, to take action, assuming this is something that's right for them. It's not right for everyone."

Lloyd nods. "There's also the flipside: those who move too quickly, too soon. But, that said, you've got to start somewhere. Even if it takes six months to get going, like it did you, all people see is the ultimate success that you've had, and not necessarily how long it took for you to get started. Developments aren't an overnight success. It takes effort at the start and, as you said, each project comes with its own relatively unique challenges, but the rewards stem from the effort you put in."

"No question", Neil says. "At this stage, I'm actually pipelining deals. I've been doing this for such a long time now that people bring deals to me instead of my having to go out and find them. Now, I can cherry-pick the ones I want to do, the real money-makers, and get them into planning. The pipeline is such that I've got sites I've exchanged on which I can move my build team on to, so the guys can get on-site and finish that one while I'm getting the planning for the next one. If that flow doesn't come through, I devise a plan B, but ultimately, I'm looking now at larger projects, eight to 15 units, and moving the team onto those. I know from experience now how long the planning will take, so I can generate that relatively steady flow where once one's finished, we move on to the next site, with smaller sites peppered in between. But back when I first took the course", Neil admits, "when we met all those years ago, I never thought I'd be at this level."

"Networking, as you said, has been a key thing in getting to where you are now. How many courses have you done to date? You came back at least six or seven times, didn't you?"

Neil laughs. "At least. I've lost count."

"And in addition to that, you've got your own local property network event in Milton Keynes, where you're based, and you do sourcing for other people, don't you?"

"We do a little bit of everything", Neil admits. "I'm delegating more now to the senior members – we've got traditional estate agencies and letting agents and qualified mortgage advisors, so we do finance and can arrange development finance for primary residential stuff. That's our bread and butter on the mortgage side. Then there's the sourcing – we find sites for clients, because there are only so many sites I can take on at one time, and the ones that don't work for me I can pass on for a fee. So, we encompass pretty much everything property related.

"I've got a building company as well", Neil adds, "which primarily services my projects. We don't do a lot of client work, beyond bits here and there, because my own stuff keeps them busy pretty much full-time. We cover most of the angles as best I can see."

"You've got a lot of angles covered now", Andi notes, "but not back in 2015, when you first came on a course. And, as you said, you came on the course five or six times, the same course with the same information, and you did it for a reason: you recognised that in that course lay a network you could build, all people who wanted to do the same thing, in one room. There were lots of people with building experience, people with funding experience, and you had an estate agency at the time. Not everyone grasps the value of that. If you're a builder and you join 45 or 50 people for three days, you can build a lot of rapport, can't you? There are a lot of future joint ventures that can get their start in that room."

Neil nods. "Absolutely. Good partnerships stem from gathering people who possess different, complementary skill sets. First of all, the course was good fun. It's not like you're sitting there, bored, for three days. Everyone engages in a good bit of banter, and the people who generally go on it are good eggs, so to speak. With my estate agent/lettings hat on, people in a build-to-let environment are going to have a load of stock at the end of it. I'm there as much to network and build relationships and help any others as well as learn. I try to add value from my experience to help others."

"It's an investment taking the course, isn't it?" Andi says. "I mean, if you're coming into the course with certain skills or service experience, there's value to be gained through building a network that provides projects, joint venture opportunities, etc. If you can obtain value equal to that of the course price you've paid, whether through work or relationships going forward, the course pays for itself. And you can take the information you learn and implement it. You can take it and literally change your life with it. It also works to mitigate the risks in a way you wouldn't if you were starting solely on your own."

"That's right", Neil says. "I used an architect whom I met on the course in a couple of my developments, one of the first courses I did. He did some of the schemes for a couple of my developments. People you meet on the course are people you learn how to work with before bringing them into any of your actual projects."

"I remember that", Andi says. "He came on a one-day course, then did the three-day course, and then joined the Mastermind, because people were buying his timber frames. He had put himself in an environment where people were doing development, and then he later progressed into doing development himself."

"I think the value of networking is really understated, especially in the developing game, because, for example, if, by going on the course, you encounter someone who has a 10-year-warranty supplier 30% cheaper than yours, that's a huge savings you've just gained", Neil says. "You don't know what you don't know, so unless you're actually talking to people and finding out what's working for them, some of the tricks of the trade, some of the methods, you're missing out on things that might translate to your own sites. You've got to get out there to find out what's happening. A lot of people get held back by fear, don't they? I'm quite happy to give it a go, really. If it's not something that poses a huge risk in my life, then I'll give it a try and see if there's a benefit from doing it."

"Something a lot of people struggle with is the financial side of developments, the purchase of the sites, the funding behind it", Lloyd points out. "You've done a lot of deals now, so can you tell us how you arrange the finance? How do you find the funding? What would you say has been key to that?"

"Well, it wasn't until I went on the first course that I learned about using other people's money in the way that White Box has structured it, so that has been integral to my success. Taking that approach, I admit, was a bit daunting to start with, not knowing how your investment proposal is going to be received, asking people for money. But, ultimately, you need to view it as you doing them a favour, because they're going to get a much better return on their investment when they're putting it with you instead of depositing it into a savings account.

"I've got a bank of investors", Neil explains, "that trust me with their money now, because they know I'm good for it, they know my track record, so it certainly is easier now than it was to start with. People close to me backed me from the start, and they've got parents and family members who are now involved. That's how I started, and after that, I began going through my list of business contacts, and that expanded my bank of investors.

"People are looking for a safe place to put their money and property is fairly safe", Neil says. "If they know you and your character, and know that you're not going to take undue risks and blow it all, they'll be more inclined to put it in the scheme, knowing that something good will come out at the end of it. You want to ensure you have clean credit, a history of always repaying your debts. Sometimes, on projects, I need to have a conversation with the investors to let them know that I might be a month or two behind, maybe due to delays with COVID, or whatever, but, ultimately, people are seeking a better place to put their money. Some people who are interested but find themselves hesitant to do developments out of fear, think, oh it can't be done without having sufficient capital. But it can be done. You can do development without any of your own money. But people do need to trust you; you've got to be a good bet for them.

"If you are someone who hasn't any experience yet, no track record, you might well struggle until you can team up with someone in the network. If you're in that situation and you've met someone through the network and you've both got knowledge and skill sets, you will be in a position to present yourself in a more favourable light. If you've got the yin and the yang, the builder and the finance guys on board, it's a different situation to just doing this on your own. I'm a big believer that if you've got the right deal, the funds will follow. If it's good enough deal, it will fund itself, however you choose to do it."

"It's being active", notes Lloyd, "getting out there and doing, like networking. I think what's been key for you, and what you're really good at, is the networking side. I think that's been a big part of your success over the last few years."

"And if you enjoy it", Neil adds, "it's not like work. It's social."

"Getting paid to go out for an evening – perfect!" Lloyd says, grinning. "Any final words of wisdom that you might have for anyone who's thinking about doing what you do?"

"Just do it! Don't think about it, just do it!" He chuckles. "'Ready, fire, aim' is one of the sayings I love that I keep hearing in the property world. You'll be waiting forever if you wait for everything to be perfect. It's never going to be perfect; nothing is. Just get out there and get it done. As they say, 'You don't have to be a great to start, but you have to start to be great'."

Lloyd nods. "That's what this book, this podcast, is all about, glimpsing how people started, how they took those first steps. A lot of the interviews are quite similar: How they got started, how they did it that first time, and figuring out what to do as they go and how to do it even better the next time. It starts with the desire to do something different, or just somewhat different, professionally. If you need to educate yourself a bit as to what to do at the start, that's always a good idea. But all you really need is the drive and a bit of a direction as to how to get it done."

"No question that the group accountability that came from participating in the Mastermind was really good for me", Neil admits. "I wouldn't be here, where I am today, if I hadn't joined the Mastermind – being in that environment, every month, with all of those people around me, witnessing what other participants were doing as well. It was really inspiring listening to their stories, as I thought, Wow, if they can pull that off, then why not me? I had been underrating what I was capable of doing, potentially. Some of the members of the Mastermind are out there doing some phenomenal things, which is a terrific motivator."

"Yes, it certainly fast-tracked your development world", Lloyd says with a smile. "Thanks so much for sharing your story with us."

DAN HULBERT & GARY SANDFORD - HULSFORD

http://www.hulsford.com/

http://www.facebook.com/hulsford

In this chapter Dan Hulbert and Gary Sandford share their story. Dan has been a good friend of White Box for a long time, having first participated in the White Box Property Developers Secrets course in 2016, after which he started looking at some decent deals. He also co-hosted the Property Developers Discovery Day with Lloyd in 2017, sharing his knowledge with others looking to get started in developments.

Dan subsequently took a short break to focus on a different property strategy, but in 2021 he teamed up with Gary to develop for the supported-living sector, providing much-needed emergency housing. They have raised millions in investment and have a very focussed business plan. Here's their story.

"Today", Lloyd says, "we welcome Dan Hulbert and Gary Sandford to the podcast. Now, our focus is about building a dream, so let's start by telling our audience what it is that you're currently doing – what you're working on, what's in the pipeline, and what you've completed so far."

"Well, from a development point of view – since we do have other property-related business", Gary begins, "we've got a factory unit that we're currently converting into six flats, we've got a house in Spalling that we've converted into two flats, a house in Boston that was converted into two flats, a piece of land in Birmingham that we're building four houses on, and a shop and upper that we converted into two flats while retaining a bit of shop at the front."

"So, about 16 different dwellings you're currently working on then? Conversions? Many of them into two flats?" Lloyd asks.

"It's bread and butter stuff", Gary says, "which we keep repeating, keeping adding more of. They're quite straightforward to sort out and complete, not too difficult to convert, given our experience. We're not really looking to go massively into developments, so keeping it fairly modest."

"Gary, what would you say is the biggest development we're looking at?" Dan, his partner, asks. "We've had a couple in the pipeline recently, but how would you sum it up?"

"No more than five or six", Gary says, with a nod.

"That's sensible", Lloyd says. "There are developers, relatively new developers, who always have an eye to do bigger and bigger deals. They start with two, three, maybe four units, and then they want to do 20, then 50. They're always chasing the next big thing, instead of remaining constant for a bit, repeating what they've done and continuing to learn at a steadier scale. If, like you, you stick with the bread-and-butter property deals, and specialize in them, you can do them over and over again, and it gets easier and easier. Especially for your contractors", Lloyd adds. "I'm sure they know exactly how it's done now – get in, get it done, make the profit, and move on to the next one."

Gary nods. "That's exactly what we do, what I call the bread-and-butter stuff, converting the three-bed house into two flats. We always buy for cash and look to recycle our money as quickly as we can. So, once planning has gone through, it's about a four- to five-week refurb. Halfway through the refurb, we apply for a mortgage and essentially recycle our money in eight to 10 weeks, ready for the next project."

"That's just brilliant", Andi says, admiringly. "Amazing. You've just nailed these down to a process. Now, Dan, you mentioned that you do other property-related stuff, outside of development. Would you give us a bit of a rundown on that as well?"

Dan nods. "So, I was already apart of White Box when I partnered up with Gary, whom I'd met through networking and Mastermind connections. I knew I wanted to do something beyond what I had been doing, but I wasn't sure what. Together, though, we started doing projects. We knew from the start that developments would be part of what we'd do, but it wouldn't be the majority of what we were looking to do.

"Gary, when we partnered, was invested in a rent-to-rent project in London, small-scale emergency housing directly to councils. He had business partners who had essentially just stumbled across it and Gary had invested in it. He explained the type of project it was and said, 'Should we look into doing this?' And we did. In just a year we've taken control of over 1600 properties in London, and we raised about £6.5–7 million in private finance to do those deals."

"That business generates a healthy six-figure monthly profit, and we're looking to roughly treble what we did in 2021 in 2022. We're up to 11 councils now, soon to be 14, and we want to get all 33 boroughs on board within three to four years from when we started." Dan smiles appreciatively. "We're on track, but we didn't expect it to go as big as it did, not so quickly. It's a good business to be in, where pretty much everyone involved wins: the investors, the councils, and, most importantly, the end users who need a place to live, which we provide. So, that's another side of what we do."

"Those figures you're talking about are impressive" Andi says. "When you started, did you actually foresee that level of profitability, the sheer scale of it?"

Dan shakes his head. "Me, personally? Absolutely not. My focus was on achieving a certain level of cash flow, and so, speaking frankly, my mindset was probably not on quite what it should have been. Gary could give you more insight into where he envisioned it could be, given he'd had some experience already."

Gary nods. "I invested in it right at the very beginning. From the day that I invested in it, I knew that I wanted to be a part of it. I didn't want to be a passive investor, although I'm probably one of the biggest investors we've got at the moment. I wanted to be more hands on – I wanted to be a part of the creation. I wanted a piece of the pie, to enjoy some of the management profit as well.

"When I first spoke to Dan about it, told him what the plan was, how we could get involved, and take some of the business, Dan was emphatic that it wouldn't work. 'Trust me', I insisted. 'It will work. It will work.'

"The first meeting we had with my other partner was about a year ago, in December 2020. I'd told Dan to just let me do the talking, that all I was going to do was to plant seeds. We weren't going to commit one way or the other. We'll come back in a month's time, I explained, and plant a few more. And, after that, then we can harvest what we've grown. And so Dan agreed. But instead of it being a hard sell to Mo, who'd gotten me to invest initially, he actually loved what I was saying, and about how we could take the business forward. We didn't have to sell him on anything. He offered it to us. He offered us the partnership."

"That's a good point", Lloyd says, "a good point to make to our audience. Some people are too focused on getting a result straightaway, but when it's business, that rush to get involved is not always the best way, is it? Instead, it's often smarter to take it one step at a time: sow the seeds, start building relationships... People invest in people. That approach is likely primarily why you achieved the results you did."

Gary nods. "And when we actually got our foot in the door, we started putting more efficient systems and processes in place, showing him how the business could be run a lot better than he'd been running it up to then. I explained how we could take this business, one that was generating probably £300,000–350,000 a year, to a level of profitability that you almost couldn't put enough noughts at the end of it.

"I said to him, 'Look, if I prove it to you over the next year that I could more than treble what you're doing now, would we be able to take more of the business?' And Mo said, 'If you do what you say you're going to do, we can talk about it'. So, we put our heads together."

"It did happen very quickly", Dan adds, "within a year. The mindset thing is definitely something you grow into. I think it was Jim Rowley who said that you've got to grow into that mindset, but you've got to believe it, otherwise you'll be standing still, you won't be moving forward. And I watched it balloon, month after month. My main job was to boost the finance and find investors, and it was just like, wow, selling itself, practically." He shakes his head with a smile. "We went from councils offering us 50- to 100-property contracts to Redbridge, which would be our biggest contract to date, who offered us 700 properties. We were like, 'Bloody hell!' We just pushed forward, putting better processes and systems in place. And at that point we had to stop focusing on buying properties and focus on this. But once we'd done that, we got building momentum, and that's when the property development projects started to roll in, as well. It definitely emphasised how important it is that when you've got an issue at hand, you really have to focus on it to be successful."

"You've certainly got to believe it to achieve it," Lloyd agrees. "You talk with ease now about 1,600 properties and £7 million in finance raised, but I'm sure it wasn't that smooth from the beginning. Would you explain where you started, how you got into property first, and when you decided you wanted to do something? How long had you been doing it for yourself as well, Gary, when you started?"

Dan nods to Gary to start.

"Well", Gary says, "back in the early days, I was a bricklayer. I went from a bricklayer to a project manager, and then to a contract manager, then to a contract director, where I was overseeing properties £100 million-plus, probably three or four of those at a time. I always say five years ago", he chuckles, "but it's more like eight years ago now."

Dan laughs. "He's the one who's supposed to be good at

numbers. It's nine years ago."

Laughter

"Okay, nine years ago", Gary admits. "For the 20 years before that, my missus was insisting that we had to do something more, that we had to increase our assets, consider buying a place to rent out. What, like a busman's holiday, I thought? Why would I want that? Work six days a week doing what I do and then doing something that I do anyway for the remaining one day a week? 'No, I'm not doing that', I said initially. But then I thought, oh, let's just do it.

"We bought our first house to rent out. It was me; Jamie, my son; and my wife. We bought our first property for £77,000, did it up, and rented it out. Then, we bought another one, refurbished it, rented it out, and then another one, same thing. Then, we bought an HMO [house of multiple occupancy], fixed that up, and rented it all out. And then we just went on scale, doing two or three at a time, doing those as joint ventures with other people. Then I went on another Mastermind – I had I don't know how many properties – it was a very big portfolio when I went to it, and since then, my portfolio has continued to increase, exponentially."

"Well, obviously, education is key", Lloyd agrees. "It's not just us who educate people in property; there are others out there, but having the knowledge and resources that come with the Mastermind program, and meeting and hearing from other people who are doing bigger things, does help drive you to do bigger and better things as well."

"I only knew one thing: Buy, refurbish, refinance, and rent out", Gary admits. "That's all I knew. I really thought that was all there was to property. I didn't know anything about PLOs [purchase–lease options], vendor finance, and all these weird and wonderful, sophisticated things that you could do with property. I didn't know about any of them. I'd just buy a property for cash, refurbish it for cash, refinance it, rent it out, and then buy another one."

Andi nods. "Sometimes, success is just about keeping it simple, and repeatable, which a lot of times is what we do on the development end of things now: keeping it within the niche, consistently turning smaller single-occupancy properties into two-flat ones... You can get really good traction on that, as you've shown." Andi turns to Dan. "Dan, how did you get started?"

"Ah, well, my dad was flipping properties back in the early 2000s", Dan explains, "when you could refinance same day and all that sort of stuff. I got involved, hands-on, then. He didn't really know what he was doing from a finance standpoint though. I've been in the building game ever since, doing refurbishments for other people and becoming a contracting company, and that went from strength to strength. Then I got educated in property probably back in 2012, 2013. That's when I realised I'd missed out on a whole heap of information, of knowledge, up to that point. And that I needed to act on it, as well, not just amass it. There are a lot of people who educate themselves, but then do nothing with it – they just keep that knowledge as education, without converting it into actual practical experience. That was my biggest catalyst, the knowledge I gained, which opened my eyes to the greater potential out there."

Lloyd nods. "Yeah, a waste of money, essentially. Why learn something if you're not going to do anything with it, not going to put what you've learned into practice?"

Dan says, "You have to not just learn it but absorb it, to look inside yourself and think about what you haven't yet done that needs doing – really take a hard, objective look at what you've been doing. It took me a while to get my head around that, but I did it. Then I started buying buy-to-lets. But I overstretched myself. I'd built a decent portfolio, but overstretched myself with the building side, I didn't have any systems and processes in place, didn't have the right team around me, etc., and so, in 2015, I nearly went bankrupt." He shakes his head ruefully. "I pretty much had to rebuild from there, from a high six-figure debt. So, I started rebuilding my processes. I set up my own network, because that's something I've always done. I had the property volt network, which I'd run for five years, and that was a good grounding for me to just completely rebuild the profile.

"Funnily enough", Dan adds, "that's how we are connected with White Box, through a mutual connection, James Burtt. I joined the Mastermind at a point where I think I was still a little bit lost, because I was still rebuilding stuff. I had a few properties still, and then, in 2017 – which is about when I joined White Box, which I did for about a year, and then had to transition away for a while, when I focused on project consultancy for investors – I ended up doing lots of HMOs for people before I realised that I needed to get back in the game, to get the mindset going again. And it was through this networking that I eventually met Gary. Bit of a roller coaster for me, mindset-wise, but, then, here we are, and I'm really enjoying the process, getting back out there and talking to people, and reconnecting to White Box.

"I like Gary's cookie-cutter approach to our business. He's a real straight shooter, tells it like it is", Dan chuckles, "which I appreciate. Our skills complement each other, which is important in one's team, one's network."

Lloyd says, "One of the things I've picked up while getting to know you over the past few years is that you jumped right onto the mentorship. You jumped into the training, fully committed, and, as you've told us, you learned something, and although you didn't necessarily apply what you learned straight away, maybe because the mindset wasn't right, as you said, ultimately you did. And that education will always be with you, should always serve you well. So, whether you do it in one year, in two years, or in three years – when you're ready – as long as you take action, what you've invested in education will pay you back 10 times, 100 times, 1000, an infinite number of times –as long as you do something. Which you have."

Dan nods. "I'm in the process of moving right now, having found our dream home and getting it on a purchase–lease option, where I get to test it out, to live in it, for three years before I decide to buy it. This isn't something I would have been able to negotiate, had I not done all the different trainings with White Box. It's helped me in so many ways, so many aspects, because it developed this mindset in me. It's not easy to execute", he adds, pointing to his head, "if this isn't working. The mindset has to be established. That's the hard part. The rest, to me, is fairly simple. But none of it would have been possible if I hadn't educated myself. I needed to understand the science of it, if you will.

"So, I think it's very important to get educated. If you want to be a doctor, you can't skip any step of the way. You have to do all the process, all the education, all the way up to your doctorate and all the rest of it. You can't just assume that I'm not going to bother going to uni. I'm not going to bother studying. It's the same thing with property, if you want to be good at something, you have to take time to study it, to educate yourself."

Gary interjects, "There's a saying that it takes 10 years to be an overnight success. People are always asking me, 'How did you build a portfolio so quickly?' And my answer is always that I had a 20-year apprenticeship, from when I started as a bricklayer, then decided I wanted to do property (which is probably more like 30 years) – that was my apprenticeship. I learned everything I needed to know in that period of time. My portfolio wasn't built over eight or nine years. I broke ground on the foundation, beginning at age 16, when I first started to work, all the way up to the present day. I try to learn something every day."

"A lot of people see what you're doing now, where you are now," Lloyd points out, "who aren't necessarily aware of what you've done over the years, and so they judge you only on that, saying, 'You're so lucky to have what you've got now.' But it's nothing to do with luck. That so-called luck is a product of all your hard work. You put yourself out there, you took risks – and there are a lot of risks involved in development. And to do something bigger involves risk, risks you've got to take, because if you don't take those risks, you'll never achieve the kinds of rewards that you've achieved."

"Absolutely", Dan says. "We look at, say, a financial loss not as a loss but as an alternate form of investment, an investment in your education. Gary taught me that. You've just learned something really valuable, and the cost of that education was the fee you needed to pay to get to the next level. Since we've been working together, Gary has always advised, 'Don't worry about the losses, because the diversity among all the various projects we have going makes the loss relatively insignificant in light of our other profitable income streams'. That's the mindset shift that you have, when you start seeing success and realising your vision.

"Networking has been a big thing", he adds. "They say, 'Network's net worth'. But something someone said to me recently, which I thought was really good, was that your network plus your self-worth is what equals your net worth. Networking won't get you anywhere, if you don't first believe in yourself."

"Me", says Gary, "I'm a planner. I know what I'll be doing over the next five years. My next five years are all mapped out in my head."

"Now, he's just gotta put it down on paper", Dan jokes.

"I can tell you where my business will be", Gary reiterates, "all of the things that I'm involved in, where they'll be in five years' time, because I will make that happen. We sat in front of our business coach, and I rattled off the five-year plan that I'd already set for our business. I'm a planner, and I'm a big fan of '10x': If I say I'm going to do £4 million, then I'm going to attempt to do £40 million. And I'll end up with £20 million", he laughs, "which will make me happy".

"These are some great successes you've achieved", Andi notes, "but there must have been some hurdles along the way. Gary, can you tell us what sorts of business challenges or difficulties you've encountered over the years?"

Gary thinks a moment.

"Well, two years ago, we had a valuation come back that was £400,000 less than we'd estimated it would be, and that was just at the beginning of the COVID-19 pandemic. It was on two shops and some flats above that we'd done. The reason was, because of the pandemic, overnight they stopped assessing any value on shops, even though our shops were leased. They had just stopped valuing them, because at the time there were about 1,500 shops every week that tenants were walking away from and not honouring their leases. So, they didn't even factor it into the valuation. I can remember speaking to you about it then, and I was nearly crying, because we had a boatload of money tied up in it. Well, four weeks later, I thought, you know what? We have that money, that value. It's not really ours; it's our investors' money, so that's not too bad. We just tell the investors that we'll be paying X amount on it, and we won't be paying a mortgage, so we'll have more money coming in every month. With that, I was over the hurt of having to tell the investors the money's being left in. I was all right with that. I was pretty happy, actually!"

"Yeah", Lloyd says, "the key takeaway from this is that is something you would never have anticipated ended up happening. At that point you have to say, okay, this has happened now, so how are we going to solve the problem? The key to your success is focusing on a solution, which is what you did by shifting your mindset about how to view the situation. In this instance, as long as the investors are happy to leave their money in, and you pay whatever per cent you'd have paid on the mortgage – e.g., commercial mortgages charge 6% interest – your investors will receive a fixed return, that interest, every year, and if they're not happy with it, another investor would be. Problem solved."

"In terms of a challenge on the building side, it wasn't really a bad thing per se, but I bought a property that was subsided, that had massive rapid subsidence, and I hadn't picked up on it. That was only a couple of years ago, wasn't it, Dan?"

"Yeah, you'd just bought it before we started working together."

Gary shakes his head in disbelief.

"It wasn't until after I bought it", he says, "that I went in and walked from one end of the property to the other, and I was stunned. I thought, what is this? I'm walking downhill!"

Leaning forward, Andi says, "When these things arise, as developers they test us. In property, as a rule, part of what you build is resilience. You assemble a toolkit to cope with problems like this. And, as Dan pointed out earlier, quoting you, it's because it's not the only deal you're doing – that it waters that down. One project will inevitably feature some issues now and again, but the ones that don't will more than make up for that."

"When I first found out about it having subsided, I thought: Underpinning – it's going to cost me a fortune! There's going to be rubbish everywhere, it's going to be dirty – it's going to be horrible! When I got back home, I went on my laptop, determined to bite the bullet and find out what lay ahead, and searched for companies that do underpinning. I found one, Geobear, which promised underpinning without disruption, that you can live in a house while they underpin it. And so I looked into that. Wasn't even expensive, as I'd feared. Cost me £9,000, and, sure enough, they literally jacked up the building with expanding foam – by 150mm!"

"That story's for another podcast, I think", Lloyd jokes.

"And when you realize you can solve those issues", Andi points out, "you can actually set up a niche, where you can solve other people's problem properties, owners who are stressed because they don't know how to solve their issue."

Gary laughs. "That is what I do now. I look for distressed properties like that!"

Dan adds, "Even the properties we've bought, the six 2-bed units, they took nearly a year just to buy, because of so many back-and-forth problems with titles and other issues. But, as Gary shared with you before we taped this interview, there are stairs and other items that could now end up potentially costing us nothing. We might even be getting the purchase price back, plus a little bit, because someone wants access through the side of the building that we've got a driveway for. It originally caused a load of headaches to get everything sorted; for example, there were numerous building conditions, planning conditions, and other items that Gary managed to iron out. It could potentially end up benefitting us. You just have to keep pushing forward and search for the silver lining."

"With everything you've learned," Lloyd asks, "between your time spent with us at White Box and your personal experience, what advice would you give to someone who's thinking about getting into development?"

Dan doesn't hesitate. "Get educated. Go and have a chat with the guys here at White Box, because they know what they're doing. Get educated, so you won't underestimate what needs to be done. Learn first, so you're going in with your eyes wide open, and only then get practical experience by going out and doing it, by buying property. Getting educated first can save you a lot of headaches. That's my advice. Gary?"

"For me", says Gary, "I'd advise taking it in baby steps. Don't dash ahead, thinking that, all of a sudden, you can become this multi-million-pound developer because it's been done by others, or because somebody else has done it in your group if you're getting educated, as there will be other people who are doing it at that level. Baby steps, start small, and work your way up. If you make a mistake on a £30,000 job, sure, it's gonna hurt a bit, but not as much as if you make the same mistake on a £3 million job. That really will hurt."

"How many years have you guys at White Box been doing development as a business?" Dan asks.

"We started in 2014, so nearly eight years", Lloyd replies.

"So, essentially, you're on chapter eight, as it were", Dan says. "Our advice to anyone starting out is not to compare Lloyd and Andi's chapter eight to your chapter one – that's as simple as it is. Learn from it, model it, and be inspired by it, but don't get ahead of yourself. And by the same token, don't get disheartened by the impressive successes of others with much more experience than you currently have and assume that you can't do it."

"And don't be attracted by that shiny penny either", Gary warns, "because that shiny penny is never that shiny when you turn it over. It's a rusty old nail."

Laughter

"Well, on that note", says Lloyd, "I know you guys do your own podcast as well, so how can people get in contact with you?"

Dan nods. "Yes, we have our own podcast, "Building on Solid Foundations", which we relaunched in February 2021, so we'd love to get you and Andi on that as well. So, people can reach out to us through the podcast or visit our website, hulsford.co.uk, and connect with us there."

Ready to Get Started?

White Box Property Solutions offers anyone the chance to start to understand the world of developments and how you can get started. We have a variety of courses and events to help you get started.

TDN: The Developers Network – Scheduled Events

A regional network event tailored to educating anyone interested in development, and hosted by those who are, themselves, actively developing properties.

PPD: Property Developers Discovery Course

A 1-day course that shares, step by step, how we, at White Box, started, why we started, and, likely what you'll find the most important to you, how we took that first step and achieved our very first development.

PDS: Property Developers Secrets Course

Our flagship 3-day course – which everyone interviewed in this book has taken, as they'll tell you. This is the course that provided them not only the fundamental education to get started but the confidence, the belief, that they were ready to start building their dream.

PDM: Property Developers Mastermind Monthly Program

Our monthly support program, designed to help those who have attended the PDS as they progress through their developments, be it their first or their first dozen. Everyone benefits from a community to help and support them through the challenges they face in their business. This is a very powerful community of developers who freely share their experience-based wisdom and knowledge on how they have achieved their goals to help you do the same.

To get started and build your dream...

Go to http://linktr.ee/whiteboxproperty